THE GOD STANDARD

By Greg & Kristen Barrett

Copyright

The God Standard

Table of Contents

Acknowledgements..4

Introduction..5

Chapter 1 – Dominion was Built Into Your Design................6

Chapter 2 – The Holy Spirit...................................13

Chapter 3 – Learning to Discern His Voice.....................19

Chapter 4 - Words of Knowledge................................30

Chapter 5 - Prophecy..39

Chapter 6 - Ministering Healing...............................48

Chapter 7 – Set Them Free.....................................56

Chapter 8 – Why Deliverance?..................................70

Chapter 9 – Spiritual Housecleaning...........................76

Chapter 10 — Prayers..87

Chapter 11 — Our Inner Healing Packet.........................91

Chapter 12 — Inner Healing Leader Instruction................109

Acknowledgements

I would like to thank, first and foremost, my husband, Greg, for supporting me through many of life's hurdles and hearing the voice of God for my life before I could even recognize His vision for me. It was more of your blood, sweat and tears that went into the creation of this book for years and I am so grateful that you have allowed me to be apart of it as a co-author.

Next, thank you to my children, Eli and Aden, for being so patient and supportive as we have grown in our gifts and built our ministry. Thank you to my parents, Mark and Barbara Creek, and to my brother, Bryan Creek, for shaping me into the woman I have become.

To our senior pastors, Derron and Lyn-Felice Calvin, I appreciate all that you continuously instill into our lives. Your support, encouragement and mentorship could not be traded for anything. To the fellow authors in our church—the Calvin's and our dear friends Mona Borgens and Donna Kenndy—I really appreciate all of the insight and guidance you have provided while writing this book.

To all of our wonderful friends, family, and Seattle Christian Church, thank you for believing in me and allowing me to take risks in my ministry even when it included traveling halfway around the world to do God's work and nursing abroad. Your prayers and spiritual covering has carried me far beyond what I could ever dream possible. Finally, I want to thank God for all that He has provided in my life. I owe everything to Him!

~ Kristen Barrett

I would first like to thank my wife, Kristen, for her unwavering support. I could not fulfill the call on my life without her constant love, faithful prayers, and endless patience. I am also deeply grateful for our sons, Aden and Eli, for choosing to pursue the call of God on their own lives.

I honor the men and women of God in my family who went before me and entrusted us with a rich spiritual heritage in Christ Jesus. Thank you, Giulio and Maria Miori, and Flora and Roy Strehlo—your lives and faithfulness did not go unnoticed. I am also sincerely thankful to Catherine Wanless, Robert Wanless, and Mike Barrett for your steadfast support and encouragement.

To the leaders who saw value in me and chose to invest in my life—thank you. Pastor Derron and Lyn Felice Calvin, we would not be where we are today without your continued grace, wisdom, and support. Pastor Vince and Jodiann Schott, thank you for the prophetic voice you have been in my life. You are truly a gift.

To my family at Seattle Christian Church, thank you for walking this journey with me, for being willing to stand with me and take risks alongside me. This has truly been a collective effort.

Above all, thank You, Jesus. You lived for me, died for me, rose again for me, and called me. May I become more like You with each passing day for the rest of my life.

~ Greg Barrett

Introduction

We are living in a time when God is once again awakening His people to a life marked by signs and wonders. This is not a distant promise or a fading memory of the early church—it is a present-day invitation. Heaven is moving, and God is calling ordinary believers to live supernaturally empowered lives.

As a husband and wife team, we have witnessed thousands of miracles over the course of our marriage, ministry and mission work. Between the two of us, we have gone on missions to various places, including Mexico, Africa, and Brazil with various organizations like Global Awakening, Amazon Outreach, Northwest University Nursing Abroad Program and our own home church, Seattle Christian Church, where we have served as associate pastors since 2009.

We leaned on the knowledge of these organizations, and others like Acts Ministry, Tim Storey, Rita and Dennis Bennett, Dr. Henry Wright and Pablo Bottari, as they have guided and shaped us as our mentors, instructors and pastors. In our book, we have compiled what we have learned over the years not only from them, but from what we have experienced in the field and at the altar.

When I was first called into the ministry of healing and deliverance as a young man of God, there were few voices to guide me and little instruction to follow. The path required faith, obedience, and a deep dependence on the Holy Spirit. I learned quickly that this calling could not be fulfilled through knowledge alone—it demanded intimacy with God and a willingness to step into the unknown.

Through that journey, I discovered that signs and wonders are not meant to be occasional events but a lifestyle. They are the natural overflow of a life yielded to God's presence and power. Healing, deliverance, and miracles are not the destination—they are the evidence of a Kingdom advancing through surrendered vessels.

As you read our book, *The God Standard*, our prayer is that something within you will awaken. May faith rise, fear fall away, and boldness be restored. May signs and wonders become woven into the fabric of your daily life as you learn to partner with Heaven, release God's power, and walk in the authority that has always been yours.

The God Standard is written by both Greg and Kristen Barrett, so you will find personal testimonies from both, told from either a man's or woman's perspective. You will hear stories from Greg of his life as a father, Marine, Real Estate Broker, Investor and General Contractor, but you will also listen to stories from Kristen as a mother, wife and Nurse. We want to show you, within this book, your invitation to embrace the standard of greatness God has already placed within you. The Kingdom is at your fingertips. Will you reach out and grab hold of it?

Chapter 1 – Dominion was Built Into Your Design

Matthew 28:19–20 records Jesus' final commission to His disciples: to go, make disciples of all nations, baptize them in the name of the Father, the Son, and the Holy Spirit, and teach them to observe all that He commanded—with the promise that He would be with us always, even to the end of the age. This was not merely a command to act; it was an invitation into partnership with God Himself.

Many believers struggle to hear the voice of God, not because God is silent, but because they are uncertain of who they are. Confusion about identity clouds spiritual clarity. If God is not seen as a good Father to a person, it becomes nearly impossible to understand oneself as a son or daughter. Without sonship, purpose remains elusive.

When people ask us about purpose, we often begin by asking about their family history—because purpose travels through bloodlines. As children of God, however, our true lineage is found in Christ. Though we were once outsiders, we have been grafted into the family of God. God's desire is not that we remain spiritual orphans, but that we mature into sons and daughters who know who we belong to.

If we are commissioned to disciple nations, then we must understand the "*co*" in the commission. "Co" means joint, mutual, and partner. Scripture tells us in 1 John 3:8 that the Son of God was manifested **for this purpose**: to destroy the works of the devil. Jesus later told His disciples, *"As the Father has sent Me, I also send you."* Though God is fully sovereign and needs no assistance, He has chosen—by His own design—to involve His children, as co-laborers, in His redemptive plan for humanity. This is the mystery and honor of sonship.

From an early age, I became aware of the spiritual realm. At just four years old, I began seeing angels and demons. I quickly realized that what I was experiencing was not safe to speak about, so I learned to carry it in silence for many years.

When I was saved at twenty-six, I understood that God was calling me out from the world. However, when I turned to the church for guidance and understanding of my spiritual experiences, I encountered rejection instead of support. My intentions were questioned, and I was told I was seeking attention. That response wounded me deeply as they couldn't understand what I was experiencing.

Caught between two worlds—no longer belonging to the world, yet not feeling accepted by the church—I began to see myself as a *misfit,* living without a true sense of belonging.

In time, I came to understand that the leaders who rejected me were responding from their own limitations. Because they could not see in the spirit, they assumed no one else could either. As God continued to lead me forward, He brought me into relationships with others like me—those who never quite fit the expected mold. The ones I once called "misfits," I now recognize as family in the Kingdom of God.

In 2018, the Lord spoke to me about an upcoming increase in the opioid epidemic in Seattle, and instructed me to begin teaching on deliverance. I agreed, even though I knew very little about the subject. Soon after, the Lord directed me to connect with a deliverance ministry in Florida and told me to get on a plane and learn more on the subject. Obedience often comes before understanding so I got on a plane and went.

As a pastor, if you had asked me whether I carried emotional wounds from my past, I would have answered confidently, "No, I'm fine—my past is under the blood." When I arrived in Florida, I expected to attend classes. Instead, I was told I would learn deliverance by personally walking through it. My first reaction was resistance. Once again, I insisted, "I'm fine." The staff gently explained that they could not help me unless I was willing to be honest. I chose to be honest and decided to go through the deliverance session.

During one session, the senior pastor entered the room, sat across from me, and said, "The Lord spoke to me about you." He said, "You call yourself a 'misfit.'" In that moment, my defenses collapsed. He continued, "God does not call you misfit. He calls you son."

That single statement shattered a lifelong stronghold. Hidden wounds of rejection and insignificance were exposed and uprooted. I wept as I felt a profound release—like a hundred-pound weight lifted from my shoulders. For the first time, I truly experienced freedom and what it truly meant to be accepted as a son of my Heavenly Father.

In that moment, I learned the difference between *doing* and *being*. My identity was no longer anchored in performance, ministry, or the approval of others, but in sonship. I could finally rest. From that place of freedom, I decided that I would never again try to fit into someone else's mold. God had formed me, accepted me, and named me His son.

There is a significant difference between servanthood and sonship. Many believers faithfully serve God yet struggle to receive their identity as His children. When your *worth* is shaped by the praise of people, it will also be dismantled by their criticism. When that feeling of rejection was uprooted from my life, I stepped into sonship—and with it came a new authority through which the power of God began to flow. Oftentimes, understanding follows obedience, arriving only after we have crossed into our promised land. What God reveals and heals within you is meant to be imparted to others, because you cannot give away what you do not first possess. This is why Galatians 5:1 says, *"It is for freedom that Christ has set us free."* The testimony of Jesus, after all, is the spirit of prophecy (Revelation 19:10).

Orphan Spirit

John 14:18 declares, *"I will not leave you as orphans; I will come to you."* The Greek word *orphanos* means "parentless"—one who has lost a parent and is vulnerable, unprotected, and in need of care. In many ways, people come to church carrying an orphaned heart.

An orphan is not only someone without a family, but also someone who has been adopted yet never feels truly included. It is possible to be born again and still live with an orphaned heart. An orphan may have a father, yet refuse to be fathered. They may have full access to love but still choose solitude over intimacy. This mindset is not rooted in abandonment, but in mistrust.

The orphan spirit describes those who possess a father but live as though they are unloved, uncovered and unseen. They resist correction, mistaking it for control, and often move from church to church to avoid relational closeness. Mentorship is perceived as manipulation, and authority is approached with suspicion rather than trust.

Jesus illustrates this in the parable of the Prodigal Son (Luke 15:11–32). One son left home to provide for himself, while the other remained but was found working in the field while the family celebrated. Though he had access to everything in his father's house, he never enjoyed it because he lived with an orphan mindset—believing he needed permission to possess what already belonged to him. Orphans rarely feel fully accepted and often operate with a poverty mindset, competing for position and resources out of fear that provision will run out. They labor to provide for themselves and call it obedience to God. The true tragedy of the orphan is not the absence of a father, but the presence of one they cannot receive.

In Luke 10, Jesus enters the home of Martha and Mary. Martha occupies herself with preparations, while Mary chooses to sit at Jesus' feet. Frustrated, Martha voices her complaint, but Jesus affirms Mary, saying what she has chosen is better. This moment exposes how orphaned hearts strive for God's approval through labor, offering Him what He never asked for, instead of living from the approval already freely given.

Mindset

It is difficult to believe that the impossible can become possible when you struggle with the person you see in the mirror. Remember, the blood of Jesus has cleansed you from the sins of your past, present and future. Because of Christ, God chooses to see you as righteous—in right standing, right thinking, and right living.

Hebrews 9 explains that in the Old Testament, the blood of goats and bulls atoned for Israel's sins, yet the people continued to live with guilty or an evil conscience. They remained "sin-conscious," even though their sins were covered. That lingering guilt was evidence that the sacrifice was incomplete and that a Savior was still needed—One who could not only forgive sin, but also cleanse the conscience. This truth is further unfolded in Hebrews 9 and 10.

Hebrews 9:14-15 (NIV) says, *"How much more, then, will the blood of Christ, who through the eternal Spirit offered himself unblemished to God, **cleanse our consciences from acts that lead to death, so that we may serve** the living God!" For this reason, Christ is the mediator of a new covenant, that those who are called may receive **the promised eternal inheritance**—now that he has died as a ransom to **set them free from the sins committed under the first covenant**."*

You cannot serve others effectively while still carrying unresolved issues from your past. When we ask someone in our church to pray spontaneously for another person, hesitation often follows. Why? Because their focus turns inward—to their own struggles—rather than outward to the person standing before them in need. If this is an area of difficulty, bring it to the cross of Jesus and place it under His blood.

Jesus died to free you from an evil conscience so that you could serve God and humanity without restraint and receive the promised eternal inheritance. What inheritance is this? It is the promise God made to Abraham and his descendants—a promise that preceded the Law of Moses. This inheritance is revealed and released through the Holy Spirit (see Galatians 3:13–14).

Hebrews 10:22 (NIV) says, *"Let us draw near to God with a **sincere heart** and with the full assurance that faith brings, having our hearts sprinkled to cleanse us from a **guilty conscience** and having our bodies washed with pure water."*

Your conscience is defined as "a **persisting notion** or belief about something." Your pattern of thought is the reality you choose to value, create and live in. If you look up "guilty" or "evil" in the Greek, you will find the word, *poneras*. In Matthew 6:13, in the Lords prayer, Jesus said to pray, *"Deliver us from evil..."* You will find the word "evil" in this text is the same Greek word *poneras* as in Hebrews 10:22. *Poneras* is defined as a life full of hardship, worthlessness, as well as being physically and emotionally sick. The root word of *poneras* is "ponos" which is great pain, laborious trouble, inevitable agony or patterns of pain. Another root word is "penes" which is poverty, toiling or a poor person. If this is what you are carrying in your heart and the reality you choose to live in, how are you ever going to receive words from God to see what He sees in you in order to empower you to break through into the impossibilities of life?

A sincere heart is a "true" heart that is cleansed by the washing of the word and the blood of Jesus or the blood of the New Covenant. John 8:32 begins, *"You will know the truth..."* This is a knowing by experience, not based on your ability to memorize scriptures. Knowledge by itself is puffed up (1 Corinthians 8:1).

You must understand the truth of who you are—your identity in Christ—before approaching God's throne of mercy and grace. Why? Because when God speaks, He is often releasing His Word—His power—into an impossible situation to bring about your breakthrough. That Word is greater than your present circumstances; it is spoken to your potential. If you cannot see the potential God has placed within you, it becomes difficult to recognize or receive a Word that is calling it forth.

If we don't allow the blood of Jesus to deliver us from our heart issues, we will be like Israel in the Old Testament, and will approach God with guilt and shame and perpetually find ourselves walking around the same proverbial mountain. Guilt is how you believe God sees you, and shame is how you will continue to respond to Him. Hebrews 4:16 tells us to come "**boldly**" to the throne of grace because we know who we are. This is important because if you don't know who you are, you will sabotage the very word(s) that will enable you to break through the impossibilities of life because you won't feel qualified to receive it.

The Beloved

After Jesus was baptized by John, Mark 1:11 (NIV) records, *"And a voice came from heaven: 'You are my beloved Son; with you I am well pleased.'"* The word "beloved" reveals priority—God loves many things, but His love for His Son is supreme. Before Jesus performed a single miracle or began His public ministry, the Father affirmed Him through love and approval.

In the very next verse, the Holy Spirit leads Jesus into the wilderness to be tempted by the devil. At the root of that temptation was identity. If the enemy can distort who you believe you are, he can entice you to misuse your authority. This was the strategy he attempted with Jesus—and it remains the same tactic he uses against us today.

He will instill lies into you until it becomes an ingrained pattern, leading you to walk right into an unrighteous belief system. As a woman with kids, when I was battling with post-partum depression after our second-born son, I felt that overwhelming urge to end my life. The enemy led me to believe that I was unworthy and inadequate as a mother, and therefore, I should just drown myself in the bath one night. Something was trying to pull me under. Thankfully, I was saved at the time (but not yet a pastor), so I knew these thoughts came from the pit of hell. I was only overly exhausted and pushed to my limits. I was able to rebuke those thoughts and set myself free. I realized at that moment, if I could strong-arm those negative thoughts and overcome those lies, then my husband and I could help others in the same manner.

Luke 4:3 (ESV) says, *"The devil said to him, 'If you are the Son of God, command this stone to become bread.'"* It's interesting to me that the devil never addressed Him as God's "beloved" Son and removed "beloved" from his statement. The enemy understands that you are unlikely to believe an outright lie. What you are far more likely to accept is a truth that has been subtly distorted. When what God has said is repeated—but not exactly as He said it—it can become a tool for destruction. The most effective form of manipulation is not blatant falsehood, but truth presented inaccurately. This is deception. Deceived people are those who have embraced a mixture of good and evil. The only way we fall is through an *almost truth*.

It was through this kind of distortion that the devil attempted to get Jesus to misuse His authority by proving Himself. Jesus had no need to do so because He knew the Father had already approved of Him before His ministry began. After the testing, Luke 4:14 (NIV) tells us, *"Jesus returned to Galilee in the power of the Spirit, and news about him spread through the whole countryside."* What was the result of His identity being tested? Power and authority.

Have you ever heard someone say, *"And you call yourself a Christian?"* That question carries an expectation—an attempt to impose a standard designed to provoke you into proving yourself. It is no different from the temptation Jesus faced in the wilderness. It is an attack on your identity meant to lure you into misusing your authority and fighting battles you were never called to fight. And a battle you are not called to fight is one you are not equipped to win.

Let me explain this further. In John 5:2, Jesus heals a paralytic at the Pool of Bethesda. Scripture tells us that there were many—possibly hundreds—of sick people gathered there, waiting for an angel to stir the waters so they could be healed. Jesus approaches one man who had been paralyzed for thirty-eight years and asks him, *"Do you want to get well?"* A few verses later, the man is healed, picks up his mat, and walks.

Acts 10:38 says of Jesus, *"He went around doing good and healing all who were oppressed by the devil, because God was with him."* This raises an important question: what about the rest of the people at the pool? How could Jesus heal "all" when He healed only one person in that moment?

The answer is found in John 5:19, where Jesus explains that He only does what He sees the Father doing. The word *all* refers to the ones that the Father directed Him to heal. Jesus was not responding to human expectation or pressure; He was moving in perfect obedience to the Father's will.

I share this because many people will hold the label "Christian" over your life, as though you must meet their expectations or prove your identity to them. You do not. As stated before, this is the same trap the enemy set for Jesus in the wilderness—tempting Him to prove an identity the Father had already affirmed. Jesus is our model.

God loved and approved of you before you took your first breath. Even while you were still in sin, He loved you enough to send His Son to the cross for you. With that truth in mind, serve, help, and heal those the Holy Spirit leads you to—no more and no less.

I encourage you to read Psalm 139, especially verse 16. Then take the entire psalm and personalize it as a spoken confession between you and your Heavenly Father.

The God Kind

Genesis 1:25–26 says, *"God made the wild animals according to their kinds, the livestock according to their kinds, and all the creatures that move along the ground according to their kinds. And God saw that it was good. Then God said, 'Let us make mankind in our image, in our likeness, so that they may rule...'"*

Adam was created in the image (or likeness) of God—the Hebrew word *tselem*, which conveys the idea of a representation or reflection of God, placed within humanity to resemble Him. The word "likeness" comes from the Hebrew *demuth,* meaning a visible resemblance, model, or form—something fashioned to mirror the original.

In Genesis 1:25, we see that all created things were made "according to their kinds." This indicates that everything on earth has a source from which it was formed. Each created thing was produced from its original kind. When we move into Genesis 1:26, we see that God Himself is the source of humanity's creation. God formed Adam by imparting something of Himself—creating humanity to reflect His nature and authority. Since everything was created from a kind or source, it is reasonable to say that Adam was created from God's own kind.

This understanding aligns with Matthew 16:18, where Jesus says, *"You are Peter, and on this rock I will build my church, and the gates of Hades will not overcome it."* The church was not built upon Peter as the foundation, but upon Jesus—the Rock, the cornerstone and capstone of life. Peter, whose name means "rock," was a stone derived from *the* Rock. In the same way Adam was created from God's kind, Peter—and all who are reborn in Christ—are brought into the God-kind through new birth.

You are gods

Psalm 115:16 declares, *"The highest heavens belong to the LORD, but the earth he has given to mankind."* This reveals a divine order: God remains sovereign over all, yet He has entrusted humanity with stewardship and authority in the earth. God is ultimately in charge, but mankind has been given responsibility and control.

Think of it this way... we own our home. When I leave, my children remain there. I am still in charge, but they are entrusted with caring for the home in my absence. Their ability to oversee it depends on how well I have taught them. In the same way, Psalm 115:16 reveals God's intent in our design and His desire for co-laboring. God is sovereign, yet He works through people who exercise the authority He has given them.

In John 10, Jesus identifies Himself as the Good Shepherd, the Door, and the Son of God. In verse 27 He says, *"My sheep hear My voice; I know them, and they follow Me."* Here, Jesus establishes both His identity and the identity of the children of God. He is then opposed by religious leaders who attempt to stone Him because they refuse to live according to the purpose for which they were designed.

In John 10:34–35 (NIV), Jesus responds, *"Is it not written in your Law, 'I have said you are "gods"'? If he called them 'gods,' to whom the word of God came—and Scripture cannot be set aside..."* Jesus is quoting Psalm 82:6–7. His point is not that humans are objects of worship, but that those who receive the Word of God are entrusted with divine authority and responsibility in the earth. When God reveals something to you, He is also granting you authority to act on it with godly authority—because grace always empowers what God commands.

Psalm 82:5–7 (NIV) continues, *"The 'gods' know nothing, they understand nothing. They walk about in darkness; all the foundations of the earth are shaken... You are 'gods'; you are all sons of the Most High. But you will die like mere mortals; you will fall like every other ruler."* This passage addresses function, not divinity. Without revelation and wisdom, people walk in darkness, and whatever shakes the world will also shake them. That was never the purpose for God's children.

If we fail to step into our calling as sons, rulers, and ambassadors, we remain powerless to confront evil and risk living no differently than those who do not know God. God's intention has always been for His sons and daughters to rule from relationship, revelation, and responsibility.

Throughout Scripture, we see the **title "god"** applied to others. This is because *God* is not a personal name but a title or office. In Hebrew, the word translated as God is **Elohim**, which comes from the root **El**—a term associated with strength, authority, and deity. We see this root in names such as **Gabriel** (*Gavri'el*), **Michael** (*Mikha'el*), and **Lucifer** (*Helel ben Shachar*). In its usage, *elohim* can refer to one who functions as a ruler, judge, magistrate, or one who exercises authority.

This understanding is reflected in 2 Corinthians 4:4 (NIV): *"The **god** of this age has blinded the minds of unbelievers, so that they cannot see the light of the gospel that displays the glory of Christ, who is the image of God."* Here, the term *god* is used to describe a governing authority influencing the present age.

We see a similar usage in Exodus 7:1 (NIV), where the Lord says to Moses, *"See, I have made you like **God** to Pharaoh, and your brother Aaron will be your prophet."* This does not imply divinity, but delegated authority. In this sense, God appointed Moses to function as a ruler or representative of His authority before Pharaoh. In Christ, this same principle applies—believers are given authority over sickness, disease, poverty, hardship, and the works of the enemy.

If *God* were a personal name rather than a title, Scripture would not apply the term to figures such as Moses, earthly rulers, or even spiritual powers. Exodus 6:3 (LSB) clarifies this distinction: *"I appeared to Abraham, Isaac, and Jacob as God Almighty, but by My name, Yahweh, I was not known to them."* **Yahweh** is God's personal name; **God** describes His office and authority in this scripture.

Created for Dominion

In Genesis 1:3, God declares, *"Let there be light,"* and light comes into existence. God looked upon a world filled with darkness, emptiness, and chaos, and He spoke not only to the problem, but to the potential within it. His words released order where there was disorder and life where there was void. In the same way, we are called through our words and actions to partner with God in turning darkness into light, emptiness into provision, and chaos into order.

Genesis 1:4–5 continues, *"God saw that the light was good, and He separated the light from the darkness. God called the light 'day,' and the darkness He called 'night.' And there was evening, and there was morning—the first day."* Notice this: God saw the light, then He spoke to it by naming it. The name gave the light its purpose.

The light did not function as *day* until God spoke it into being. Romans 4:17 reminds us that God *"gives life to the dead and calls things that are not as though they were."* God alone has the authority to assign purpose to His creation. When we learn to see people as God sees them and speak over them what God says, the purpose of their design is awakened, and they begin to walk in who they were created to be.

Genesis 1:26 (NIV) declares, *"Then God said, 'Let us make mankind in our image, in our likeness, so that they may rule...'"* God created Adam and Eve with a divine assignment: to rule the earth in partnership with heaven, exercising authority on earth as God exercises authority in heaven.

Training for Reigning

Genesis 2:19 says, *"Out of the ground the LORD God formed every beast of the field and every bird of the air, and brought them to Adam to see what he would call them. And whatever Adam called each living creature, that was its name."*

God brought the animals to Adam and entrusted him with the authority to name them. Because of Adam's relationship with God, the Lord knew Adam would perceive the same purpose and potential in creation that He Himself had placed there. When Adam exercised his authority by naming each creature, the name established its function and identity.

This pattern of partnership is echoed in God's relationship with Jeremiah. In Jeremiah 1:11–12, the word of the Lord comes to the prophet: *"Jeremiah, what do you see?"* When Jeremiah responds, *"I see an almond branch,"* the Lord replies, *"You have seen well, for I am watching over My word to perform it."* God was not testing Jeremiah's eyesight—He was confirming that Jeremiah could perceive what God was about to bring to pass. God is searching for people who can see the potential He sees and have the courage to declare it.

Amos 3:7 (NKJV) reinforces this truth: *"Surely the Lord GOD does nothing, unless He reveals His secret to His servants the prophets."* The word "nothing" means exactly that—*no thing*. God is not limited by humanity; He could act alone. Yet, in His Sovereignty, He has chosen to work in partnership with people, revealing His intentions so they may speak, act, and agree with Him on the earth.

The Jesus Style

Acts 10:38 (NKJV) says, *"How God anointed Jesus of Nazareth with the Holy Spirit and with power, who went about doing good and healing all who were oppressed by the devil, for God was with Him."*

This verse offers an apostolic summary of how Jesus impacted the world so powerfully. The opening phrase—*"how God anointed Jesus of Nazareth"*—emphasizes His humanity. Jesus is the eternal Son of God, uniquely qualified to make the once-for-all payment that canceled the power and debt of sin for humanity. Fully God, He became fully man. As God, Jesus did not need the anointing; it was His humanity that required the anointing of the Holy Spirit and power.

Here, *power* is not something added to the Holy Spirit, but the emphasis within the phrase. We see this pattern elsewhere in Scripture. For example, Matthew 6:33 instructs us to seek first the Kingdom of God *and His righteousness*, with righteousness carrying the emphasis. Romans 14:17 tells us that the Kingdom of God is righteousness, peace, and joy in the Holy Spirit—revealing that righteousness is central to how the Kingdom is lived out. In the same way, the book of Acts highlights *power* as the defining expression of the Holy Spirit's work through Jesus.

The way Jesus operated in the miraculous is not meant to impress us as spectators, but to serve as a model to follow. If Jesus performed miracles solely as God, we could admire Him without expectation. But when we understand that Jesus did the impossible as a *man* fully yielded to the Holy Spirit, remaining passive is no longer an option. Jesus ministered in power because He was anointed with the Holy Spirit and power.

The Holy Spirit is the One who reveals the Father's will and activity. In John 16:13–15, Jesus explains that the Spirit will guide us into all truth, speaking only what He hears and revealing what is to come. First Corinthians 2:11–12 tells us that the Spirit knows the thoughts of God and freely makes them known to us. This explains how Jesus could say, *"I only say what I hear My Father say, and I only do what I see My Father do"* (John 5; John 8). It was the Spirit of God revealing the Father's heart and actions to Him. Because of this perfect alignment, He could truthfully say, *"Anyone who has seen Me has seen the Father"* (John 14:9).

After His resurrection, Jesus promised that the Holy Spirit would not speak on His own authority, but would take what belongs to Jesus and make it known to us (John 16:13–14). This revelation is essential to walking in the grace and power of God. We will explore this further in a later chapter. Acts 10:38 (NKJV) says, *"How God anointed Jesus of Nazareth with the Holy Spirit and with power, who went about doing good and healing all who were oppressed by the devil, for God was with Him."*

Beyond the many sick at the Pool of Bethesda, Scripture also records a paralyzed man at the Beautiful Gate in Acts 3—someone Jesus Himself had walked past. Later, it was Peter and John that prayed for this man, and he was healed. I mention this because many people build theology around what *did not* happen rather than giving glory to God for what *did* happen. Jesus never taught on unanswered prayer because He did not experience unanswered prayer. He did only what the Father told him to do. It was not His responsibility to heal that paralyzed man, but for Peter and John to work in signs and wonders in that moment. When we learn to tune into God and act only on what He says, we remain in faith rather than drifting into presumption or foolishness.

Jesus defined ministry by what we cannot do on our own, but only with God. Matthew 10:8 (NKJV) records His instruction: *"Heal the sick, cleanse the lepers, raise the dead, cast out demons. Freely you have received, freely give."* If these things were possible through human strength alone, there would be no need for God. We are called to the impossible so that we live in dependence on Him—cultivating both humility and an effective prayer life. God *commands* us to heal, cleanse, raise dead, and cast out demons under his authority.

When Jesus says, *"Freely you have received, freely give,"* it also reminds us that we are not the end result of our prayer life. Other people are. Our prayers are meant to release God's power and grace into the lives of those He places before us.

Chapter 2 – The Holy Spirit

Galatians 3:29 (NLT) declares, *"Now that you belong to Christ, you are the true children of Abraham. You are his heirs, and God's promise to Abraham belongs to you."* Likewise, Galatians 3:13–14 (ESV) explains that *"Christ redeemed us from the curse of the law by becoming a curse for us... so that in Christ Jesus the blessing of Abraham might come to the Gentiles, so that we might receive the promised Spirit through faith."*

The death of Jesus on the cross did not reconnect us to the Law of Moses, but to the covenant God established with Abraham (see Genesis 12:2–3; 17:2–10). Without the Holy Spirit, we cannot fully receive the inheritance that began with Abraham. When the Holy Spirit speaks and works in our lives, He is reconnecting us to those very promises God made long before the law was given.

Ephesians 1:13–14 (KJV) states, *"After that ye believed, ye were sealed with that Holy Spirit of promise, which is the earnest of our inheritance..."* In real estate terms, *earnest money* is a deposit made by the buyer to confirm a contract—a guarantee that the full payment is coming. In the same way, the Holy Spirit is God's guarantee in our lives, confirming that what He has begun will be brought to completion. Receiving the Holy Spirit is evidence that more of God's inheritance is yet to come.

Jesus affirmed this in John 16:7 (NKJV): *"It is to your advantage that I go away; for if I do not go away, the Helper will not come to you; but if I depart, I will send Him to you."* The active work of the Holy Spirit in our lives stands as evidence of Jesus' resurrection and ongoing Lordship.

In John 14:16 (ESV), Jesus says, *"I will ask the Father, and he will give you another Helper, to be with you forever."* The word *another* is *allos* in Greek, meaning "another of the same kind." Just as replacing a part in a vehicle requires a like-kind component, this passage reveals that the Holy Spirit is not different in nature or purpose from Jesus. He is the exact same and He continues the ministry of Christ in us and through us.

From Heaven to Earth

When we are born again, we inherit the *"great and precious promises"* that make us *"partakers of the divine nature"* (2 Peter 1:3–4). First Corinthians 2:12 (NIV) explains, *"What we have received is not the spirit of the world, but the Spirit who is from God, so that we may understand what God has freely given us."* The phrase *freely given* is the language of inheritance. An inheritance is freely received, not earned—it is the benefit of another one's labor. As Galatians 3:13–14 makes clear, it is because of Jesus that we now have access to the promises given to Abraham. These promises become active in our lives through the work of the Holy Spirit, received with an attitude of honor.

Jesus explained this process to His disciples in John 16:12–15 (NKJV): *"I still have many things to say to you, but you cannot bear them now. However, when He, the Spirit of truth, has come, He will guide you into all truth... He will glorify Me, for He will take of what is Mine and declare it to you."* Jesus was revealing how the resources of heaven are transferred into the life of a believer.

It is through the voice and declaration of the Holy Spirit that the promises of the Kingdom are deposited into our lives. Whenever God speaks, His prophetic anointing is released within His word. Prophecy does not merely predict the future; it creates the same reality here on earth as it is in heaven (see Romans 4:17). God's word always carries the power to accomplish what it declares. Therefore, we must position ourselves to hear His voice. Our ability to hear the Lord is directly connected to the value we place on the Word of God actively working in our lives.

Hearing the Voice of God

The first step in hearing the voice of God is unconditional surrender of the heart. Obedience is simply saying *"yes"* to the Holy Spirit before He ever speaks. We are called to trust the Lord, not based on what we understand or what we see, but on who He is (see Proverbs 3:5).

In Luke 1:31, the angel Gabriel tells Mary that she will conceive and give birth to Jesus. The intension, of course, is that this would happen through a virgin birth by the Holy Spirit—something that had never occurred before. Naturally, Mary asks, *"How?"* Zechariah asked a similar question in Luke 1:18, yet he was struck mute until John was born because his question was rooted in unbelief. At first glance, it may seem that Gabriel does not answer Mary's question—but he does. In Luke 1:37 (NKJV), he declares, *"For with God nothing will be impossible."*

In the Greek, *nothing* is rendered as *"no thing."* The word "thing" is *rhema*, meaning a freshly spoken word from God—a present-tense word released by His living voice. The word "impossible" means *without ability*, and at its root is *dunamis*, God's power and ability. A literal rendering of the verse would be: *No freshly spoken word from God will ever be given to you without the power necessary to accomplish it.* In other words, grace always enables what it commands.

Jesus affirmed this principle in John 6:63 (NKJV): *"It is the Spirit who gives life; the flesh profits nothing. The words that I speak to you are spirit, and they are life."* Jesus spoke only what He heard from the Father through the Holy Spirit. John 12:50 (AMPC) reinforces this: *"Whatever I speak, I am saying exactly what My Father has told Me to say."* When Jesus spoke, the Spirit of God was released into the situation, and the life of the Kingdom manifested—because the Kingdom of God is expressed through the Holy Spirit (see Romans 14:17).

When we speak what the Holy Spirit is saying—through gifts of revelation such as words of knowledge—our words carry the same spiritual substance. When we declare something *in the name of Jesus*, it is as though Jesus himself is standing beside us making the same declaration. when we align with God, the Holy Spirit empowers our words, and they become *spirit and life*. These declarations do not merely describe God's reality; they help create it.

When God issues a declaration, the power to fulfill it is released simultaneously. This is why, when words of knowledge are given from the altar, the ministry team is instructed not to strive or over-pray. The word has already been released, and the power to heal or deliver is present. Our role is simply to help people receive what has already been made available—often through prayer or the laying-on of hands if the breakthrough has not yet manifested.

Through our relationship with the Holy Spirit, we are called to be God's redemptive answer to the problems of the earth—by hearing His voice and manifesting the Kingdom of God on earth as it is in heaven.

Romans 14:17 tells us that the Kingdom of God is expressed through the Holy Spirit. When Adam chose to obey the voice of the devil, the Holy Spirit (and the dominion that came with Him) departed from Adam. From that moment on, everything Adam had been created to rule began to rule over him. The Holy Spirit will not dwell upon what is unclean, and His manifest presence in our lives stands as evidence that Jesus was raised from the dead (see John 16:13).

Adam was placed on the earth as the original steward—what Scripture later refers to as the "god of this world." His first assignment was to exercise authority over the serpent that had been cast down, seeking to reclaim power. Without spiritual life, humanity remains subject to the god of this world. A person may gain the whole world by aligning with that system, but like Adam, they forfeit their soul in the process. To walk in freedom, we must return to a dominion mindset that begins in the spirit.

John 4:24 (NIV) declares, *"God is spirit, and his worshipers must worship in Spirit and in truth."* The Psalms teach us that God inhabits the praises of His people (Psalm 22:3). Just as God once walked with Adam in the cool of the day, He still delights in dwelling within the praise of His church. When you lift yourself in worship, you begin to see from God's perspective—His truth, His ultimate reality. Conversely, when you embrace a lie, your perspective becomes distorted.

You become like what you worship. Psalm 115:4-8 NASB says, *"Their idols are silver and gold, The work of man's hands. They have mouths, but they cannot speak; They have eyes, but they cannot see; They have ears, but they cannot hear; They have noses, but they cannot smell; They have hands, but they cannot feel; They have feet, but they cannot walk; They cannot make a sound with their throat.* **Those who make them will become like them, everyone who trusts in them**.*"*

How do you know what you worship? Evaluate what occupies your thoughts most often. What you continually think about reveals what you value, and what you value is what you worship. When Jesus is not at the center of your thought life, worship has been misplaced.

Worship opens the door to the realm of the spirit. Whatever you worship, you gain access to—but it also gains access to you. This applies to both good and evil. The danger is that once a door is opened, you cannot always control what enters, whether that access was intentional or unintentional. And it may be hard to close those doors once they have been opened.

This principle is clearly seen in the life of someone struggling with anxiety. Anxiety and worry are forms of meditation—specifically, meditation on fear. Jesus tells us not to worry (Matthew 6:25), and Mark 4:24 instructs us to, *"consider carefully what we hear."* Proverbs 23:7 reminds us, *"As a man thinks in his heart, so is he."* The Lord once spoke it to me this way: *"What you continually think about is what you will eventually bring about."* Because of this, we must actively guard our heart and take every thought captive, making it obedient to Christ (2 Corinthians 10:5).

Working Together For Good

Romans 8:28 (NIV) declares, *"And we know that in all things God works for the good of those who love him, who have been called according to his purpose."* What God desires to accomplish in the earth, He chooses to accomplish in and through His people. You cannot fulfill your assignment apart from God, and God has chosen not to fulfill His purposes in the earth apart from you.

Proverbs 8:24–31 (NKJV) offers a powerful picture of the Holy Spirit's role in creation:
"When there were no depths I was brought forth,
When there were no fountains abounding with water.
Before the mountains were settled,
Before the hills, I was brought forth;
While as yet He had not made the earth or the fields,
Or the primal dust of the world.
When He prepared the heavens, I was there,
When He drew a circle on the face of the deep,
When He established the clouds above,
When He strengthened the fountains of the deep,
When He set a boundary for the sea,
That the waters should not transgress His command,
When He marked out the foundations of the earth,
Then I was beside Him as a **master craftsman**;
And I was daily His delight,
Rejoicing always before Him,
Rejoicing in His inhabited world,
And my delight was with the sons of men.*"*

This passage reveals that the Spirit of God was actively involved in every stage of creation—rejoicing not only in the work of the creation of this world, but in humanity. The same Spirit who partnered with God in creation now partners with believers to bring Heaven's purposes into the earth.

There are no limitations on what the Word of God can create in your life. Romans 4:17 reminds us that God *"gives life to the dead and calls those things which do not exist as though they did."* If God can release a word to heal a headache, He can release a word to heal cancer. If He can speak life into a weary body, He can speak strength into paralyzed limbs. The limitation is never God's voice—it is our willingness to receive, believe and respond.

In 2017, three trusted men of God independently released the same word over my life. As a man of God myself, I was also instructed by the Spirit of God to create an additional source of income. At the time, I was working full-time in real estate and doing quite well, so I initially struggled to understand why another revenue stream was necessary. As I searched my own heart, real estate felt like the only area where I had experienced real success and confidence. I told the Lord that I wanted to return to flipping properties—something I loved and believed could naturally produce additional income.

However, I never received confirmation from the Lord to flip properties. Instead, I continued to pursue Him. About a year later, my pastor prayed for me, and the Holy Spirit spoke a clear, specific, and unmistakable word. The challenge wasn't clarity—it was qualification. God spoke to something He said I was qualified for, yet I felt completely unqualified to do it. The Holy Spirit instructed me to obtain my general contractor's license and start a flood restoration company—an industry I knew nothing about.

Despite my hesitation, I obeyed. In a short period of time, the business grew rapidly as I built teams of contractors to restore homes damaged by flooding. Not long after that, I said to the Lord, "You never answered my prayer about flipping houses." The Lord responded, "Yes, I did. Do you have people who can work on homes?" I replied, "I do now." In that moment, I realized God had answered my prayer—but He answered it His way, not mine (see Isaiah 55:8–11). He filled that need with the tools and resources I hadn't realized it would require to accomplish this goal.

But going back, my sense of feeling unqualified ran deeper than that assignment itself. When my parents divorced around the time I was fourteen, I carried a belief that I had never been taught essential "man-skills" needed for my future. Because of this, I struggled so deeply with the idea of becoming a general contractor, so the Lord led me to Exodus.

In Exodus 25:8–9, Moses is instructed to build a sanctuary for the Lord, including the Ark of the Covenant, the golden lampstand, the table of showbread, intricate curtains, and the bronze altar—tasks Moses himself was not qualified to complete. Exodus 31:2–6 (NASB) reveals how God solved that problem:

"See, I have called by name Bezalel… and I have filled him with the Spirit of God in wisdom, in understanding, in knowledge, and in all kinds of craftsmanship… In the hearts of all who are skillful I have put skill, that they may make all that I have commanded you."

Could they fulfill their assignment before the Spirit of God came upon them? No. Could they fulfill it afterward? Absolutely. This shows us that fulfilling our God-given purpose requires partnership with Him. We must allow Jesus to speak into our hearts and equip us for what we cannot accomplish on our own. Often, God speaks directly to areas we have overlooked or avoided because we have little faith in those places. Yet faith comes by hearing, and hearing by the word of God (Romans 10:17).

Romans 8:26–27 (NASB) explains this partnership beautifully:

"In the same way the Spirit also helps our weakness; for we do not know how to pray as we should, but the Spirit Himself intercedes for us with groanings too deep for words… according to the will of God."

Intercession means standing in the gap—not merely praying *for* someone, but praying *as* someone who is aligned with God's heart. When we pray in the Spirit, we pray in union with Him. Our spirit aligns with His Spirit, and our will comes into agreement with His will. Through this kind of intercession, God works all things together for the good of those who love Him and are called according to His purpose.

Personal Tongue

1 Corinthians 12:8–10 describes nine gifts of the Spirit, often called gifts of revelation. Of these nine, praying in the Spirit—or speaking in tongues—is the only gift we can initiate ourselves. I often compare this to Ezekiel 47, where the prophet steps into water that is first ankle-deep and then progressively deeper. When we initiate this gift, we begin praying in the Spirit with what we know, and the Holy Spirit meets us there. As we continue, we sense Him partnering with us, taking the lead, and drawing us into deeper waters. When we

are seeking to hear the Holy Spirit more clearly, we often have worship playing in the background to keep focus on Him as we begin praying in the Spirit.

In 1 Corinthians 14:4, it says, *"The one who speaks in a tongue edifies himself, but the one who prophesies edifies the church."* It is important to speak in tongues in order to initiate hearing the voice of God, but it is even more valuable to possess the gift of the Spirit of prophecy to encourage and guide others.

In 1 Corinthians 14:5, Paul says, *"I wish that all of you could speak in tongues."* Why? So that we might be built up, brought into alignment with the will of God, and positioned for all things to work together for our good. Tongues are beneficial for personal prayer and spiritual strengthening. But Paul says prophecy is greater in the church setting. Tongues without interpretation build up an individual, whereas prophecy (the interpreted tongues) builds up everyone.

As noted in Romans 8:26–27, when we pray in tongues, it is not our natural mind praying; our spirit is praying the language of heaven from a place of surrender. In that posture, we give ourselves over to His will. In 1 John 5:14–15 tells us that when our prayers align with God's will, He not only hears us, but we can have confidence that we will receive what we ask.

A.W. Tozer once said, "The hard work of prayer is getting yourself into a state of mind in which you prefer the will of God over your own." God will not answer a prayer that contradicts His will for our lives. When I pray in English, I am expressing my thoughts and desires—praying from the outer part of my being, the soul, which includes my emotions and intellect. But true prayer flows from the spirit. When I pray in tongues, I pray in the language of the Spirit; my words are emptied of self, free from my own agenda and limitations. Often, we want to pray, but we are wrapped up in ourselves and our problems. Praying in the Spirit bends my will to His, allowing Him to pray in me and through me. It is an act of surrender that declares, "Not my will, but Yours be done."

Praying in the Spirit helps quiet the left side of the brain—the part anchored in logic, analysis, and reasoning. I often refer to this as the "flesh zone." When you pray in the Spirit, you lean into the right side of the brain, which is the creative, intuitive, and receptive side of your brain. It is in this place that we connect with the God of the impossible. What the Holy Spirit speaks is often sudden and beyond our natural ways of thinking or understanding. If we fail to shift into this posture in prayer, the words God speaks can fall into our blind spots and be easily dismissed. The more you pray in the Spirit, the more you open yourself to the creative nature of God, and the more your faith is strengthened.

The prophetic is not predictable. Living from the left-brain mindset can keep believers from stepping out in faith and can hinder them from receiving a word for healing or breakthrough. In Genesis 12:1–3, God told Abraham to leave his country, his people, and his father's household and go to a land He would show him. The flesh always looks for order and certainty. We want to move only within what we understand, so when God speaks, our natural response is often, "Give me clarity, and then I'll go." But God's response is usually, "Go, and I will give you clarity." When we posture ourselves in this manner, we will find ourselves waiting on God and He is actually waiting on us.

Jude 1:20 says, *"But you, beloved, building yourselves up on your most holy faith, praying in the Holy Spirit."* I have found that praying in the Holy Spirit is a powerful faith builder because it moves me out of my own intellect, logic, and reasoning and opens me to the realm of the Spirit. In that place, I step into God's reality—where there are no boundaries or limitations, and where the impossibilities of life begin to look possible.

Impartation

In Acts 19:6, we read, *"And when Paul had laid his hands on them, the Holy Spirit came on them, and they began speaking with tongues and prophesying."*

When we reach this point while teaching our classes, we often ask for a show of hands from those who have not yet received the gift of the Holy Spirit with the evidence of speaking in tongues. With the help of the class, we then lay hands on those individuals for the impartation and infilling of the Holy Spirit with the evidence in praying in tongues. When this happens, it is common to hear testimonies not only of spiritual breakthrough, but also of physical and emotional healing.

It is also important to observe how long it takes people to release fear, logic, and reasoning—the pull of the left side of the brain—and step into the open, creative posture of faith. This is one of the greatest challenges we encounter at the altar. We often refer to it as getting people out of the "flesh zone." Kristen came up with a convenient acronym to help define what keeps people locked into that *flesh zone:*

F: fear

L: logic

E: emotions

S: stagnation

H: hinderance

This "F.L.E.S.H. zone" is the area that you want to keep their minds out of in order to connect their spiritual ears to God when you are imparting God's restoration onto them.

Chapter 3 – Learning to Discern His Voice

Renewing the Spirit of Your Mind

This chapter is designed to help you receive from the Holy Spirit. Most of us would agree that we are strong in faith in certain areas and weaker in others. If, as Romans 10:17 says, *"faith comes by hearing,"* then the issue is often not a lack of faith but a difficulty in hearing or discerning God's voice. Revelation is God's job and clarity is ours. When an unresolved wound anchors our appetites of fleshly habits, it becomes especially hard to hear God clearly in that area of life. In those moments, the temptation is to replace hearing God with "feeling our way" through Christianity and labeling our emotions as God's voice—even when He is not speaking in that area at all.

You may hear God clearly when it comes to healing, yet struggle to hear Him regarding finances or relationships. Because of this imbalance, we often live out of our strengths and quietly ignore our weaknesses. I have found growth in multiple areas of my life by first submitting my strengths to God, trusting that my weaknesses would follow. We are conditioned to bring our weaknesses to God, but I would encourage you to begin with your strengths. From there, take the principles that work in your areas of strength and apply them to the rest of your life. If a gift functions effectively in one area, it can function in all areas.

The first step in hearing the voice of God is positioning your heart with a "yes" before He asks a question or makes a request. God is a good Father, and His thoughts toward you are to prosper you, not to harm you—to give you hope and a future (Jeremiah 29:11). To carry a genuine "yes" in our hearts, we must believe that God has a destiny prepared for us, and that we cannot move into our future while clinging to the unresolved issues of our past.

Romans 12:2 reminds us, *"Do not be conformed to this world, but be transformed by the renewing of your mind, so that you may prove what the will of God is—His good, acceptable, and perfect will."* As our minds are renewed, our ability to hear, discern, and respond to God's voice becomes clearer, and we begin to walk confidently in His purposes for our lives.

Identifying Your Source

Everyone is aware of the internal and external thoughts and voices speaking to them, but many struggle to discern their source. We tend to listen to the voice of what we value most—whether good or bad—and disregard voices we deem unimportant. Scripture gives us a clear example of this in Matthew 16. When Jesus asked, *"Who do you say that I am?"* Peter responded, *"You are the Christ, the Son of the living God."* Jesus blessed him and identified the source of that revelation as the Father. Yet only a few verses later, when Jesus revealed that He would go to the cross, Peter protested, saying, *"God forbid it, Lord! This shall never happen to You."* Jesus immediately rebuked him, *"Get behind Me, Satan! You are a stumbling block to Me; for you are not **setting your mind** on God's interests, but man's."* Jesus identified the source of Peter's words as Satan—not because Peter was evil, but because his thinking was rooted in human reasoning rather than the life of the Kingdom (see Romans 8:6–8).

This raises an important question for all of us: are we discerning our own voice, the enemy's voice, or God's voice? Divine thinking is the ability to access the mind of Christ. As 1 Corinthians 2:16 says, *"We have the mind of Christ."* We must evaluate each voice we hear, and ask ourselves, is this edifying and encouraging? Or is this thought disheartening or discouraging? There lies the answer of who is truly speaking into you in that moment. Let us go into it a bit further...

Every voice you hear will sound like your own. The challenge is discerning its source. The Holy Spirit speaks uniquely to each person, communicating in a way we can understand. Your natural voice tends to reason logically—one plus one equals two. The voice of the Holy Spirit, however, strengthens, encourages, and comforts (1 Corinthians 14:3). Often, I recognize God's voice because it comes suddenly—a spontaneous thought, impression, or image that seems to appear out of nowhere. Even when it surprises you, it is accompanied by peace. You have to remember that God speaks to your future or your potential as if it already happened. Even when God is speaking to you, it can be easy to dismiss His voice, because God sees you as He sees His Son—complete and perfect in Him. When you struggle to accept the person you see in the mirror, it becomes difficult to see yourself as God sees you, and even easier to undermine the future He desires for your life. When you realize who you are, you will be the person He called you to be and fulfill the very purpose you were created for.

The enemy's voice is easier to recognize because it is rooted in fear and turns your focus inward, distorting your faith, identity, and perspective. Jesus said in John 8:44 that the devil is a liar and the father of lies; there is no truth in him. For some, this manifests in night terrors or intrusive thoughts—attempts by the enemy to plant deception. If you examine what the enemy is trying to convince you of and reverse it, you will often discover the very will of God for your life.

2 Peter 1:3–4 reminds us that God's divine power has given us everything we need for life and godliness through knowing Him. Through His precious and magnificent promises, we become partakers of the divine nature and escape the corruption of the world caused by sinful desire.

God has fully equipped each of us to live a godly life and fulfill the purpose of our existence. To walk in that reality, however, we must be willing to crucify false appetites, misplaced securities, and unhealthy desires—things we may have unknowingly attached ourselves to and even labeled as "God." Only then can we clearly discern His voice and live from the life of the Kingdom.

We are spiritual beings with a soul, living in a physical body. Our spirit was designed to commune with God and think like Him. Our soul—our mind, will, and emotions—was designed to interact with the world. We often talk about IQ (Intelligence Quotient), our capacity for logic and reasoning, and EQ (Emotional Quotient), our ability to process, manage and respond to emotions—both others and your own—known as empathy. Both are rooted in the natural person. But we also possess a Spiritual Quotient (SQ): the capacity to think in alignment with God through the Spirit. SQ is recognizing or having awareness of values and purpose of life. Having a deeper understanding of your SQ will allow an inner peace during hardship and the ability to improve your EQ.

Emotional Encumbrances

Wherever there is an original, there will always be a counterfeit. The enemy does not bother counterfeiting what has little value. For example, you will never see fake one-dollar bills circulating widely. Counterfeits are made from what is valuable, like hundred-dollar bills. The presence of a counterfeit proves that an original exists. After nearly thirty years in the church, I have witnessed many accurate prophetic words come to pass. I have also seen relationships, businesses, and finances collapse because someone "felt" something was God when it was not. There is a significant difference between feeling and hearing—especially when the source is not rightly discerned.

Proverbs 22:29 reminds us of the importance of discipline and discernment, and it continues with a sober warning about appetite and self-control. The realm of the senses, if not submitted to the Spirit of God, can become a breeding ground for sin. As we explained before, the enemy understands that the most effective form of manipulation is not an outright lie, but a truth that is slightly distorted. This is deception—a mixture of good and evil that leads people astray through an "almost truth." Satan made death appear desirable to Eve before the first sin ever occurred. Spiritual warfare often involves making evil seem reasonable, so that disobedience looks like obedience. What many call "common sense" can be the most dangerous kind of thinking, because it produces only common results.

When appetite drives your life instead of purpose, your ability to serve and influence leaders is compromised. Romans 8:5–6 explains that those who live according to the flesh set their minds on what the flesh desires, which leads to death, while those who live according to the Spirit experience life and peace. This is why Jesus sharply rebuked Peter when Peter tried to dissuade Him from going to the cross. Peter's perspective was rooted in personal attachment, while Jesus' mission was rooted in redemption for all humanity.

Peter wanted Jesus to remain with him; Jesus wanted to be with all of God's children forever—and that required the cross and the sending of the Holy Spirit.

Romans 8:5–8, as rendered in the Mirror Study Bible, highlights that our thought patterns reveal their source. A mind dominated by the senses gravitates toward spiritual death, while a mind anchored in the Spirit experiences life and peace. Flesh-based thinking and Spirit-led faith stand in opposition. It is impossible to accommodate God's desires while remaining immersed in self-centered appetites. Faith—not flesh—defines who you are.

Wisdom requires that we recognize the appetites within us that could compromise what God desires to release through our lives. We must know our strengths and weaknesses, and in areas of weakness, we need support. Let me give you a practical example. For two months, I searched for a specific blue Toyota Tundra truck—a color only produced in 2019 and extremely rare. When I finally found one available in the next state over, I was told it had already sold. I was deeply disappointed. A few days later, Kristen said to me, "The Holy Spirit told me your truck is nearby. Check again." I dismissed it at first, but when I checked online, that exact truck had just been listed only thirty minutes from our home. Today, it sits in my driveway.

Why couldn't I hear the voice of God in that moment? Because my disappointment stole my attention. I was emotionally attached to the first outcome and missed the voice of God for another opportunity. My wife, who had no emotional investment in the situation, heard clearly. Emotions did not cloud her spiritual ear like it had done to me. Interestingly, this occurred after a church service where I had prophesied and released words of knowledge for healing—yet I couldn't hear the voice of God for my own need. When you feel you are not hearing the voice of God, hang out with people who do (see Matthew 10:40–41). Oftentimes, when we are attached to our outcome, we are viewing life through a tunnel when God has put people in our lives who can see from a broader perspective.

The first sin in Scripture illustrates this principle clearly. Genesis 3:6 tells us that Eve saw the tree was good for food, pleasing to the eye, and desirable for gaining wisdom. Her decision was driven by sight, desire, and appetite. Often, we label our desires as "God" simply because they feel good or seem right. But God will always place more than one option before the heart, and He gives us the freedom to choose. When the heart is pure, discernment comes easily. When the heart is wounded or encumbered, it becomes difficult to distinguish truth from counterfeit.

Many believers can hear God clearly in certain areas—such as healing—but struggle in others, like finances or relationships, due to unresolved wounds. Past financial loss, trauma, or rejection can cause us to rely on feelings instead of the voice of God. In those areas, we may act from emotional need rather than divine direction, missing the grace God intends to provide.

Living by feelings alone is dangerous, especially when those feelings are shaped by unhealed wounds. Jeremiah 17:9 warns that the heart is deceitful above all things, while Matthew 5:8 tells us that the pure in heart will see God. When we protect wounds instead of surrendering them, we prevent God from speaking freely into our lives. This lack of trust can become a spiritual stronghold that requires deliverance. We must admit to having those wounds and bring them before the Lord for restoration. Denial will only cause the wound to grow and multiply.

1 John 2:16 reminds us that the lust of the flesh, the lust of the eyes, and the pride of life do not come from the Father but from the world. The Greek word *epithumia*—translated as "lust"—refers to strong desire or longing. That desire can be holy or destructive, depending on its source.

This is why the path Jesus invites us to walk is narrow. It requires discernment, surrender, and a heart purified by the Spirit, so we can recognize the original and reject the counterfeit. We grow and mature in discernment through its constant use (Hebrews 5:14).

The Narrow Road

Matthew 7:13-14 says, *"Enter through the narrow gate. For wide is the gate and broad is the road that leads to destruction, and many enter through it. But* **small is the gate and narrow the road that leads to life, and only a few find it.***"*

Being a former Marine, I keep a lensatic compass on my desk—a tool designed for land navigation—and I often use it as an illustration for understanding God's direction for your life. I have relied on a compass while navigating the hills of California, the triple-canopy jungle of Panama, and Japan's Northern Training Area. Anyone who hikes through unfamiliar terrain knows the importance of carrying both a map and a compass. Together, they help you stay oriented when the path is unclear. In the same way, God has ordered your steps. Yet, just as with Eve, the enemy will question what God has said and offer an alternative in order to distance you from God, delay your purpose, and divert your direction. The Bible is your map; the voice of the Holy Spirit is your compass.

A compass contains 360 degrees, meaning there are 360 possible directions you could take. But only one degree—one azimuth—will lead you directly to your objective. Being off by just one degree may seem insignificant at first. Yet after 300 feet, that single degree puts you sixteen feet off course. After a mile, you are nearly one hundred feet away from where you were meant to be. In dense terrain like a jungle, being one hundred feet off your path can feel like being one hundred miles away, making it extremely difficult to find your path or destination. This is how easily following the wrong voice, emotion, or impulse can pull you far from God's intended course for your life. As Jesus said, the gate is small and the road is narrow that leads to life, and few find it.

Proverbs 14:12 warns, *"There is a path before each person that seems right, but it ends in death."* When appetites and feelings are not governed by the Spirit of God, they subtly redirect us—one degree at a time—onto paths that lead to destruction. When we attach our hearts to inferior desires, we forfeit the superior life we were created to live.

Let me ask you a question about land navigation: is it easier to navigate during the day or at night? Most would say daytime. Surprisingly, that's not always true. Although visibility is better during the day, what you see in the natural can be deceptive—it constantly changes and can lead you off course. Night navigation, on the other hand, forces you to rely entirely on your equipment. Instead of trusting what you see, you trust your compass and map. In the same way, what we see in the natural often contradicts what God is doing in the Spirit.

Isaiah 55:9 reminds us, *"As the heavens are higher than the earth, so are my ways higher than your ways and my thoughts higher than your thoughts."* When our experiences do not align with God's Word or His voice, we are tempted to navigate using inferior tools—our emotions, appetites, and reasoning—which lowers the standard of life God has called us to and pulls us off course. In navigation, missing your first objective places you out of position for the next one, and every subsequent decision after an initial error only compounds the mistake. At times, God allows us to walk in darkness so that we become fully dependent on our equipment—His Word and His Spirit. That dependence keeps us on course and enables us to reach our destination without unnecessary delay.

Course Correction

When Jesus corrected Peter about his mindset, He revealed how to realign one's course. He continued by saying, *"If anyone wishes to come after Me, he must deny himself and take up his cross and follow Me. For whoever wishes to save his life will lose it; but whoever loses his life for My sake will find it"* (Matthew 16:24–25). Most people set their minds on their own interests because they are seeking security but our trust in God will allow Him to direct our path (Proverbs 3:6).

This is why Jesus addressed worry in Matthew 6:25–33. People worry about their lives—what they will eat, drink, or wear—because of a desire for security. Instead of pursuing the voice of God, worry over perceived lack disrupts our ability to hear Him clearly. In response to Peter's mindset, Jesus called him to release his own interests, because God had a far greater plan in mind. Release always comes before increase. When you cannot see the full picture, obedience may initially feel like loss, but God's intent is always to add to you—for His purpose and for yours.

If you sense that you are off course from your God-given purpose, one of the most effective ways to realign is through mentorship within your local church. From the day I walked into church, I intentionally sought out coaches and mentors. Matthew 5:5 says, *"Blessed are the meek, for they will inherit the earth."* Meekness is not weakness; it is strength submitted under authority. It means being teachable and coachable. In other words, "Blessed are the teachable, for they will inherit everything." An inheritance is receiving what someone else labored for, and honor is the key that unlocks it. Through mentorship and faithful stewardship, God has appointed a season of maturity as to when your inheritance will be released (see Matthew 10:40–41; Galatians 4:1–2).

Pursuing mentorship opens the door to wisdom. Proverbs 4:7 tells us that the first step of wisdom is to acquire it, and Scripture consistently affirms that wisdom is found in a multitude of counselors (Proverbs 11:14; 15:22; 24:6). When emotional encumbrances hinder your ability to hear God's voice, the Holy Spirit will often speak through people who love you, guiding you back into the grace and direction God has prepared for your life.

Purification Before Power

Matthew 5:8 declares, *"Blessed are the pure in heart, for they will see God."* The opposite is also true: areas of impurity will blind us to the things of God. The word *pure* comes from the Greek *katharos*, meaning spiritually clean—purged, purified by God, and free from the contaminating influences of sin. A mind or heart governed by the appetites of the flesh cannot be trusted, but one governed by the Spirit can.

Scripture often describes the purification of the heart as a refining or smelting process. Malachi 3:2–3 says, *"But who can endure the day of His coming? And who can stand when He appears? For He is like a refiner's fire or a launderer's soap. He will sit as a refiner and purifier of silver; He will purify the Levites and refine them like gold and silver. Then the LORD will have men who will bring offerings in righteousness."* When people approach God with impure motives or attitudes, He lovingly takes them through a process of refinement so their hearts can be made righteous and aligned with Him.

John the Baptist echoed this truth in Luke 3:16–17 (NKJV): *"I indeed baptize you with water; but One mightier than I is coming… He will baptize you with the Holy Spirit and fire. His winnowing fan is in His hand, and He will thoroughly clean out His threshing floor… but the chaff He will burn with unquenchable fire."* Chaff represents worthless philosophies and mindsets—things that carry no spiritual nourishment.

This refining theme appears throughout Scripture and if you resist it, you will not mature. Even Jesus had to learn obedience through what He suffered (Hebrews 5:8). Isaiah 1:25 (NIV) says, *"I will turn my hand against you; I will thoroughly purge away your dross and remove all your impurities."* Likewise, Isaiah 48:10 declares, *"See, I have refined you, though not as silver; I have tested you in the furnace of affliction."* God's refining work is not meant to destroy us, but to remove what blinds us so we can clearly see Him and walk in His ways. The enemy has long tried to use affliction as a weapon to destroy us.

Affliction is defined by the Oxford Dictionary as "something that causes pain or suffering." In Hebrew, the word for "affliction" is *oniy*, meaning poverty or hardship. It comes from the root *anah*, which carries the ideas of pain, misery, frustration, and depression.

Through pain or affliction, God often allows the impurities of the heart to rise to the surface. One of the clearest ways to recognize pain in a person is by listening to their words. Jesus said, *"For out of the abundance of the heart the mouth speaks"* (Luke 6:45). In the smelting of gold, impurities rise to the surface as the metal is heated. In the context of deliverance, I often say, "What comes up wants to come out." Our responsibility is to recognize these impurities when they surface and respond with repentance. Repentance is like a ladle that removes the impurities from the heart. This process may need to be repeated several times until the pain connected to the issue is fully healed.

If mentorship or the refining process alone does not bring course correction, I recommend going through deliverance. Deliverance creates space for others walk you into your freedom and to help you discern what the Holy Spirit wants to address. We will explore this in greater detail later in the book.

Prophetic Dimension

Habakkuk 2:3 (NIV) declares, *"For the revelation awaits an appointed time; it speaks of the end and will not prove false. Though it linger, wait for it; it will certainly come and will not delay."*

Isaiah 46:10 (NIV) echoes this truth. God makes known the end from the beginning and declares from ancient times what is still to come, saying, *"My purpose will stand, and I will do all that I please."*

God is invested in what you might call "spoiler alerts." He is less concerned with you simply watching the story unfold and more interested in you knowing the outcome before the journey even begins. Prophecy is God's spoiler alert—it reveals the destination so you can walk with confidence toward it.

Worry enters a person's life when they believe their end is uncertain or threatened. God, however, is eternal. He is not only present at your beginning but already standing at your end, guiding you toward it and delighting in the journey He takes with you.

Jeremiah 29:11 (KJV) affirms this: *"For I know the thoughts that I think toward you, saith the LORD, thoughts of peace, and not of evil, to give you an expected end."*

You are called to run your race and fulfill the purpose for which you were created. God's plan for you is one of increase. When He says His thoughts are "not of evil," there is a reason for that emphasis. One meaning of evil is "adversity," and when you pursue the path God has designed for your life, you will often go against the grain of what is commonly accepted—both inside and outside the church. Scripture tells us that the fruit of following Jesus will bring a hundredfold increase in this age, along with persecutions (Mark 10:30). Even so, remember this: God is good, and He can only give what He possesses—and that is His goodness. Anytime God births something new in you, there will be persecutions. This happened when I first began ministering healing and it happened again over the subject of deliverance.

We Hear What We Value Most

The **Principle of First Mention** teaches that the first information we receive about a subject will shape how we perceive it from that point forward. In other words, what we hear first becomes the lens through which we interpret everything else related to that topic. All future experiences are filtered through that original understanding. When our children hear truth from us first, they are better equipped to face a world filled with deception, because they already have a framework of truth in place through which they can process what they encounter (see *Spiritual Intelligence* by Kris Vallotton, pp. 26–27).

The **Reticular Activating System (RAS)** is a network of neurons located in the brainstem that plays a key role in arousal, awareness, and motivation. Its primary function is to filter information and store what we determine to be valuable. What we consider unimportant is often ignored or forgotten, falling into our "blind spot." This process can work for us or against us. The RAS forms neural pathways in the brain, making certain thought patterns easier to access. The more often a thought is repeated, the wider and more established that mental "highway" becomes. When we renew our minds through revelation from the Holy Spirit, new neural pathways are formed and strengthened by the attention we give them. In this way, our sense of value directly shapes whether our mindset becomes constructive or destructive.

Here are a few examples of how the RAS functions. While traveling with my family, I walked into an arcade filled with over a hundred video games from different eras, all producing loud and competing sounds. Almost immediately, I said, "I hear *Dig Dug*!"—one of my favorite games growing up as a young boy. Out of all the noise in the arcade, how could I identify that one game playing in the back? The answer is *value*. I associated success and enjoyment with that game, so my brain (or my RAS) was trained to pick up on it, even in a noisy environment.

Another example involves our son, Eli, involving our Jeep Wrangler. Jeep drivers often acknowledge each other with what's known as the "Jeep wave." Before he started driving the Jeep, I asked him how many Jeep Wranglers he noticed on the road? He said, "Not many." Then, I asked how many does he notice now that he is driving? He replied, "Dad, they're everywhere." What changed? Value. Once driving the Jeep became meaningful to him, his awareness shifted.

Discerning the voice of God works the same way. Turning your RAS onto God by simply valuing Him and His word first, will allow you to recognize His presence in your surroundings. Unfortunately, as discussed earlier, people can place more value on their wounds and false appetites than on God's voice, which makes it difficult to hear Him clearly. Jesus warned us to *"consider carefully what you hear"* (Mark 4:24), because you can tune into the wrong things, and just glaze over what God is trying to speak into you. There is a difference between merely hearing something and truly perceiving it. Faith is meant to be the lens through which we see everything through.

Finally, the RAS can also function negatively. Unresolved traumas/wounds—for example, those connected to rejection—can shape what we tune in on and how we interpret life. These wounds may originate from experiences such as emotional trauma during pregnancy, a difficult birth, feeling unwanted, parental disappointment over gender, early divorce, abandonment, sibling rivalry, or various forms of abuse—verbal, physical, or sexual. Even one of these experiences can plant seeds of rejection that influence perception, often without us even realizing it.

Rejection is the *perceived* denial of love. When it goes unaddressed, it continues operating quietly in the background of a person's life and becomes the lens through which future relationships are viewed. At our core, we all have a deep need to be loved. When a spirit of rejection is ingrained in us, we can unknowingly gravitate toward relationships we were never called to and relationships for which we have no grace for. In those moments, a person may "feel" they have confirming words from God and label the relationship as God-ordained because their Reticular Activating System (RAS) has been trained to attach value to anything that validates how they feel as that rejected child.

That person may genuinely be a Christian and hear the voice of the Holy Spirit clearly in certain areas of life yet struggle to discern God's voice in the area of rejection. In that wounded place, the need for affirmation from people can carry more value than the voice of a loving Father. As a result, God's voice is not discerned in that area and falls into a personal "blind spot." Most of us have blind spots—areas of our life where hearing God is difficult. Wisdom calls us to recognize these weaknesses and avoid making decisions in those areas, without godly counsel. Allow trusted, mature believers to hear God for you where you fall short. They can help guide you on the right path. As Scripture teaches, wisdom is found in a multitude of counsel.

Romans 12:2 speaks of the renewing of the mind. To discern God's voice above every other voice, we must give it greater value than anything else in our lives (Matthew 6:33). When God's Word and voice hold the highest value, it becomes the most recognizable voice we hear, no matter how many others compete for our attention. One of the remarkable features of the RAS is that what we do not value is often discarded and quickly forgotten.

For example, I once had a friend insist that he had beaten me at ping-pong—also known as table tennis. I responded honestly and said, "I don't remember that." He was sincere, but I truly couldn't recall it. Years earlier, I had made a decision to value my victories and forget my losses. Your mind will filter your memories based on what you choose to value.

2 Corinthians 10:5 says, *"We are destroying sophisticated arguments and every exalted and proud thing that sets itself up against the true knowledge of God, and we are taking every thought captive to the obedience of Christ."* To experience true transformation, we must confront our past and the "truth lens" through which we have viewed life and be willing to admit that some of what we believe may not actually be true. This requires a great deal of humility. As we renew our minds to the nature of God, we replace faulty first impressions with spiritual truths—combining spiritual thoughts with spiritual words.

Jesus said in Mark 10:15, *"Anyone who does not receive the kingdom of God like a child will never enter it."* We are called to reset our truth lens with childlike trust by renewing our minds and establishing a new Principle of First Mention. How do we do this? We repent for believing the thoughts about ourselves that God does not believe, and we choose to believe in our hearts that we are deeply loved by Him. His word over our lives becomes the only true reality.

Jesus said in John 8:31–32, *"If you continue in My word, then you are truly disciples of Mine; and you will know the truth, and the truth will make you free."* The word "truth" here is *aletheia* in the Greek, meaning "reality." As we meditate on God's Word, it retrains our mindset—defining what is real, what is false, what is valuable, and what should be discarded.

Flow in the Spirit

Ezekiel 47:6–12 (NIV) describes a river flowing from the presence of God, bringing life everywhere it goes. As the water moves toward the Dead Sea, the salt water is healed and becomes fresh. Wherever the river flows, living creatures multiply, fish abound, and life flourishes. Fruit trees line both banks, bearing fruit every month, their leaves providing healing and their fruit providing food. Yet the swamps and marshes remain salty because the water does not flow through them.

This river represents the flow of the Holy Spirit. The Spirit brings life, healing, and restoration to everything He touches. What flows into you through the Holy Spirit was never meant to stop with you—it was designed to flow through you and out of you. When there is no outflow, life stagnates. This is why the Dead Sea is dead: the Jordan River flows into it, but nothing flows out. Jesus said, *"The words that I speak to you are spirit, and they are life"* (John 6:63). You are not meant to be the final destination of your prayer life—others are. When you speak what the Spirit is saying, what is dead in and around you comes back to life.

Jesus echoed this truth in John 7:38–39: *"Whoever believes in me… rivers of living water will flow from within them."* He was speaking of the Holy Spirit, who would be given to those who believe. The life of God within us is meant to overflow.

When I tune into my heart, I tune into that flow—the river of God within me. Flowing thoughts become His voice. Flowing images become His vision. Flowing emotions reflect His heart. I choose to live from the condition of my heart rather than relying solely on my intellect or strength. The moment I choose worry, I allow the enemy to influence my thought life, apart from God, and step out of the flow and come under the influence of a lie.

Ephesians 1:17 says, *"I keep asking that the God of our Lord Jesus Christ, the glorious Father, may give you the Spirit of wisdom and revelation, so that you may know him better."* This kind of knowing requires intimacy, because revelation without wisdom lacks purpose. Revelation is truth unveiled; wisdom is the ability to apply that truth. One definition of wisdom is, "skill in managing affairs." Revelation exposes what God is saying, but wisdom makes that revelation relevant in real life.

Joseph is a clear example. Through revelation, he discerned what was wrong with Pharaoh's economy. Without wisdom, revelation is irrelevant. It was through wisdom that Joseph provided a strategy that allowed an entire nation to flourish during famine and created a pathway for his promotion. Wisdom is free, but revelation will cost you—it demands responsibility and stewardship.

Think of it this way: when you purchase a lawn mower, the operating manual comes at no extra cost. In the same way, wisdom is readily given. Revelation, however, requires honor. Honor is an investment that grants access to the deeper things of God. With revelation comes a burden of responsibility, so we must understand our role in what God reveals and how to steward it well. God never gives revelation without also providing what is needed to manage it, which is why Scripture urges us to ask for wisdom (James 1:5).

Ephesians 1:18 continues, *"I pray that the eyes of your heart may be enlightened."* You were created in the image of God, and your mouth speaks from the overflow of your heart (Luke 6:45). A heart that has been purified can be trusted. This is a mind set on the Spirit—a posture that leads to life and peace (Romans 8:6).

Receiving From God

Habakkuk 2:1–3 says, *"I will stand at my guard post and station myself on the watchtower; I will keep watch to see what He will say to me, and how I should respond when I am corrected. Then the Lord answered me and said, 'Write the vision and make it plain on tablets, so that the one who reads it may run. For the vision is for an appointed time; it hastens toward the goal and will not fail. Though it seems slow, wait for it; it will surely come and will not delay.'"*

To hear the voice of God (for ourselves or our church), we intentionally create an atmosphere that allows us to hear. This includes an environment of worship, where focus is centered on Jesus. Worship is what allows me to "clear the mechanism" and rid myself of any distractions that would prevent me from receiving from God. There are a few key postures that help to receive:

Submission: *"I will keep watch to see what He will say to me"* (Hab 2:1). This means coming before the throne of grace with an open heart, laying down every care so the Holy Spirit can minister in any area He chooses. We all know the places our hearts are attached—material things, relationships, finances, opportunities, fears, or ambitions. We have to be willing to place all of our heart issues at the cross in order to receive from the Holy Spirit with childlike trust.

Stillness: When I desire to hear from God, I go to a place that is free of distractions and have worship playing in the background. Worship helps quiet my soul, surrender my thoughts, and align my heart with the Holy Spirit. It anchors my affection in Him and allows me to remain at my "guard post," attentive and at rest.

Seeing: Hearing requires seeing. If I can see it, I can seize it. I fix the eyes of my heart on Jesus so I can "watch and see." Whether my physical eyes are open or closed, I intentionally make room within my heart to receive. As I relax in His presence, visions, impressions, or pictures may come as I pray.

Hebrews 12:1–2 reminds us, *"Let us throw off everything that hinders and the sin that so easily entangles. And let us run with perseverance the race marked out for us, fixing our eyes on Jesus, the pioneer and perfecter of faith."*

Ephesians 1:17 (Mirror Study Bible) says, *"I desire that you will draw directly from the source; that the God of our Lord Jesus Christ, the Father of glory, kindles within you the spirit of wisdom and revelation in the unveiling of his master plan. I long for you to know by revelation what he has known about you all along."*

Ephesians 1:18 continues, *"I pray that the eyes of your heart, flooded with light, will enable you to grasp the magnitude of his glorious intent in identifying you in him—so that you may know how precious you are to him. What God possesses in your redeemed innocence is his treasure. You are his portion, the sum total of his inheritance."*

Finally, learn to **picture** what God is saying. A picture is worth a thousand words. Meditate on the stories of Scripture and imagine what is happening. In Joshua 1:8 says, *"Keep this Book of the Law always on your lips; meditate on it day and night..."* Meditate is *hagah* in the Hebrew and means "to imagine." Meditation engages imagination, and imagination is rooted in creativity. Genesis 1:27 tells us we were created in the image of God, which means God saw us before He formed us. Godly imagination is simply choosing to see what God says is true.

Genesis 15:5–6 says, *"The Lord took Abram outside and said, 'Look up at the sky and count the stars— if indeed you can count them.' Then He said to him, 'So shall your offspring be.' Abram believed the Lord, and He credited it to him as righteousness."* This was important as a dark sky represented human limitation and the stars represented a divine revelation of a future generation that would come from God and birthed through Abraham and Sarah. Because of this, imagination and vision were mandatory.

Remember, you are God's delegated authority on the earth (Psalm 115:16), and God does nothing without first revealing His plans to His servants the prophets (Amos 3:7). In the Old Testament, this revelation often came through prophets, but under the New Covenant, this continues through the children of God, who hear His voice (John 10:27).

Once you see what God is saying, the next steps are simple but powerful: believe what He says, speak what He says, and move in what He says. As 2 Corinthians 4:13 and Psalm 116:10 declare, *"I believed, therefore I spoke."* When you speak God's word, it becomes established in your heart. Job 22:28 (AMP) affirms, *"You will also decide and decree a thing, and it will be established for you; and the light of God's favor will shine upon your ways."*

Finally, faith must be expressed through action. James 2:26 reminds us that *"faith without works is dead."* Whenever God speaks, He releases His grace—His favor and supernatural ability—empowering you to walk out what He has declared.

Suddenly

Learn to recognize God's thoughts as sudden (flowing) thoughts. As mentioned earlier, a pure heart is formed through a refining process—a furnace of affliction that removes misplaced appetites and unhealthy attachments. This purification allows us to see Jesus as He truly is and to see ourselves as God created us to be. When God speaks, His voice often comes as a sudden thought that settles upon the heart and mind. It can also be described as a sudden awareness accompanied by deep conviction. *Sudden* means, "*happening quickly and without warning.*" God's words are always spoken in love and come to strengthen, encourage, comfort, and at times correct with loving guidance—but never to condemn. His voice brings peace, not shame.

When I say God's voice comes suddenly or spontaneously, I literally mean it often catches me by surprise. I've compared it to pulling into an intersection and being struck by a car from a direction I never saw coming. Many times the Holy Spirit will engage with me right when I get up. I may wake up in the morning and suddenly hear a worship song that resonates within me, I may have an impression of a Bible verse or I may see or get a word about a person or situation. Oftentimes, this is the "suddenly" I receive to help me step into His presence.

In contrast, sudden thoughts that originate from the world or the enemy are rooted in the lust of the flesh, the lust of the eyes, or the pride of life (1John 2:16). The fruit of those spontaneous thoughts is fear or pride-based, which makes their source easier to identify. Analytical thoughts—those rooted in logic and reasoning—are usually your own thoughts.

When we tune into the flow of the Spirit, we can hear His thoughts and His voice. When we tune into flowing pictures or impressions, we receive visions. When we tune into His emotions, we feel His heart and am moved with compassion. Seeking the face of Jesus requires laying down every care and opening all my senses to Him. The Holy Spirit speaks in many ways, but in this context, we encourage you to open your eyes, ears, and emotions—God may speak through one, two, or all three.

Words create atmosphere, so we always begin prayer time by approaching Jesus with thanksgiving. From there, we expand our prayers to include reading and declaring scripture, praying for family, extended family, church, and others. It is in the place of prayer and thanksgiving that we pause, relax, turn my full attention to Jesus, and wait for Him to speak—through sight, sound, or emotion. At times, we may suddenly see a person's face. Other times, we may hear Him address an issue that we need to surrender over to Him. Sometimes, we simply feel how Jesus feels toward us. We remain in that place until we sense He has finished speaking.

As you learn to recognize and respond to God's voice in your private life, you will find yourself increasingly quick to discern His voice and step into His flow when ministering to others.

Journaling: Communicating with God

Journaling is one of the keys to learning how to step into the flow of the Holy Spirit. I began journaling by writing words and Bible verses on index cards so I could keep God's promises and my purpose continually before me. Kristen has a notebook that she journals and records dreams in. During seasons when we felt under attack, we could return to our journal and those cards as a reminder of truth, a source of strength, and a hiding place in God. Journaling trains your mind to be set on the Spirit and helps you move from the left side of the brain—logic and reasoning—into the right side, which is more open, creative, and receptive.

There are several prophetic streams, but in this section, we will focus on one of them. First Chronicles 29:29 says, "*From beginning to end, they are written in the records of Samuel the seer, the records of Nathan the prophet...*" Here we see two prophetic expressions: the seer and the prophet. The Hebrew word for prophet is *nabiy'*, which means "to bubble up" or "to flow forth." The gifts are the same in nature but different in expression. The *nabiy'* prophet is one who accesses the "suddenly" of God and steps into His flow in order to release what He is saying. We will explore this more fully in Chapter 5.

We have found that journaling is one of the simplest and most effective ways to step into the flow of the Holy Spirit. Before we read the Word of God, we ask the Holy Spirit to enlighten the eyes of our heart

(Ephesians 1:18). When a phrase, verse, or idea seems to illuminate or stand out on the page, we pause and ask the Holy Spirit how it applies, and then we begin to write. As we write, we intentionally silence the analytical part of our mind that craves structure, spelling accuracy, or perfectly formed sentences. There will be time to edit later. Now is the time to just scribble down what you hear or feel. This is where Romans 8:6 comes into play—setting the mind on the Spirit brings life and peace.

Another helpful practice is to ask the Holy Spirit a question and then set your attention on Him. Ask something simple, such as, "Lord Jesus, why do You love me?" Then, begin writing or typing whatever comes to you, without overthinking it. You may produce a sentence, a paragraph, a page, or several pages. You will know when He is done speaking to you. When we journal, we simply tell myself to start writing and trust that the Holy Spirit within will guide what is written.

When you finish, review what you wrote and make sure it aligns with Scripture. When we teach this in a classroom setting, we often ask students to first ask the Lord why He loves them, journal what they hear, and then, we ask students to share with us what they heard God saying about them. Other times, we ask the students what they may hear God is speaking about their fellow classmates. Time and again, we have seen how accurate these impressions can be.

I remember one instance when I wrote the phrase "Xena the Princess Warrior" about a woman in the class. When I asked her what it meant, she looked stunned and said, "As a little girl, I always wanted to be Xena the Princess Warrior." Often, you may receive words, pictures, impressions, or emotions that don't immediately make sense to you—and that's okay. When ministering to others, ask them what it means to them and allow the Holy Spirit to reveal what He is trying to communicate to that person.

We use the same principle in our ministry at the altar. Many people try to analyze what the Holy Spirit is doing, and in doing so, they unintentionally block their own breakthrough. I once asked the Lord why nothing seemed to happen when I prayed for certain people, and it was because they were too focused on their intellect and reasoning to receive from the Spirit. To help them disengage from that mindset, I would give them simple instructions—such as leaning forward, leaning back, or taking a deep breath—while I laid hands on them. This occupied their minds just enough for the Holy Spirit to move, and breakthrough would often follow.

Hearing the voice of God can be as simple as quieting yourself, fixing your spiritual ears on Jesus, tuning into spontaneity, and writing. Turn on worship music, sit comfortably with Him, and tell Him that you love Him. Pause, then write what you see, hear, or feel. Ask Him why He loves you. Pause, again, and write what you receive. Afterward, test the word by comparing it with Scripture or submitting it to a trusted mentor or coach. As 2 Corinthians 13:1 says, *"By the mouth of two or three witnesses every word shall be established."*

The more you journal, the more quickly you will learn to step into the flow of the Holy Spirit when ministering to others. Over time, this practice will sharpen your accuracy in prophetic journaling and help you grow into the gift and function as a *nabiy'* prophet.

Chapter 4 - Words of Knowledge

"And the disciples went everywhere and *preached, and the Lord worked through them, confirming what they said by many miraculous signs*" (Mark 16:20, NLT).

Several years ago, I was invited to a church in Priest River, Idaho, to do a Power Show. The event included feats of strength, preaching the gospel, and an altar call where we prayed for the sick. I was standing in the back of the church while my friend Jimmy was up front igniting the audience. At one point he boldly declared, "Greg will be praying for the sick, and everyone is going to get healed."

When I heard that, my faith turned inward and doubt began to sink in...and honestly, I started looking for the nearest exit. The level of expectation placed on me felt overwhelming. I quietly asked the Lord, "Are You going to show up?" I wasn't expecting an answer, so I was surprised when I clearly heard the Holy Spirit say, "It depends. Are you going to open your mouth and speak?" I responded, "Yes." He replied, "You do your job, and I'll do Mine."

That moment clarified everything for me, as the burden to muster greater faith or produce signs and wonders lifted. Our role is simply to speak the word and will of God; His role is to confirm what is spoken. This is what it truly means to co-labor with God. The healings and miracles were so impactful that the church members asked us to remain there while they went into town to bring back more people in need of healing.

Job 22:28 (AMP) says, *"You will also decide and decree a thing, and it will be established for you; and the light [of God's favor] will shine upon your ways."*

Over the years, I have seen many miracles. I once prayed for a friend who had been paralyzed by a stroke, and he was completely healed—walking out of the hospital the same day. The hospital documented it as a medical miracle. I have witnessed tumors and blood clots disappear, cancer healed, the deaf hear, and much more. For a long time, I saw the Holy Spirit heal someone every few weeks, but it was rarely through a word of knowledge. Instead, I would see a need, muster my faith, and believe God to meet the need.

While I had always known that healing was God's will, the more I focused on my own faith, the more aware I became of what I believed I lacked, and the more hesitant I was to pray for the sick. That focus created pressure. Everything changed when I personally received healing through a word of knowledge.

I used to experience episodes of shortness of breath that felt like fluttering in my chest or an irregular heartbeat. One Sunday morning, I was sitting in the front row at church when our senior pastor said, "Jesus is healing someone who has a heart condition. It feels like a fluttering in your chest." I hadn't even told my wife about this issue, even though Kristen is a nurse and would know what to do about it. When he spoke that word, I lifted my hands and received my healing. Instantly, the sensation in my chest stopped, and I knew Jesus had healed me.

My first thought was, "How did he know about my condition?" My second thought was, "I want God to use me in this way to bring healing to others." From that point on, I began pursuing information on words of knowledge. I bought *The Essential Guide to Healing* by Bill Johnson and Randy Clark. I didn't even read the entire book yet—I went straight to the chapter on words of knowledge. As soon as I received the revelation, I felt the Holy Spirit immediately activate the gift in me.

There are nine gifts of the Spirit. As 1 Corinthians 12:8–9 (NKJV) says: *"For to one is given the **word of wisdom** through the Spirit, to another the **word of knowledge** through the same Spirit, to another **faith** by the same Spirit, to another **gifts of healings** by the same Spirit, to another the **working of miracles**, to another **prophecy**, to another **discerning of spirits**, to another **different kinds of tongues**, to another the **interpretation of tongues**."*

A word of knowledge is a spiritual gift in which God supernaturally reveals information through the Holy Spirit—information that could not be known by natural means. There is a strong connection between words of knowledge in healing and prophesy. For this section, we will focus on words of knowledge for healing.

The purpose of a word of knowledge is to generate faith in the atmosphere. The more specific the word, the greater the faith it releases among those involved. Words of knowledge often work in partnership with the gifts of healing and prophecy. Jesus said He could do nothing on His own, but only what He saw the Father doing (John 5:19–20). The same principle applies to us. The key to revelatory gifts is learning to recognize what God is doing. When you perceive His activity, understand that you did not arrive at it on your own—it was revealed by God as an invitation to join Him in bringing life into places of darkness.

In healing ministry, the word of knowledge is given to you, while the healing is released to the person you are praying for. In the same way, words of knowledge and discerning of spirits often work alongside prophecy—the word of knowledge and discernment are for your understanding, and the prophetic word is for the person receiving ministry.

1 Corinthians 2:12 says, *"Now we have received, not the spirit of the world, but the Spirit who is from God, so that we may know and understand the things freely given to us by God."* One of the primary roles of the Holy Spirit is to reveal what belongs to Jesus and to freely make it known to us. When we look at Galatians 3:13–14, we see that Jesus' death on the cross brought us into His righteousness, granting us access to the blessing promised to Abraham. That same passage also states that the Gentiles would receive the promise of the Spirit through faith. This is significant, because the Holy Spirit speaks on behalf of Jesus and freely reveals what has been given to us by God. What has been given? The promises made to Abraham.

In the previous chapter, we learned that God's voice often comes as a sudden awareness or a sudden flowing thought. In Scripture, this is sometimes referred to as a *"rhema"* word. A rhema word is an active, spoken word from God—a present or "now" word that reveals what is available in the moment. When the Holy Spirit speaks, He is "now" making the resources of heaven accessible to you. Let's look at a few examples in the Bible.

Romans 10:17 says, *"So faith comes from hearing, and hearing by the word (rhema) of Christ."* Faith does not come merely from routine reading; this verse shows that faith is birthed out of relationship—out of hearing God's voice.

I apply this principle not only to words of knowledge, but to everyday life. Faith comes by hearing His voice. When churches emphasize that we simply need "more faith," the focus shifts to our ability rather than His. What we truly need is not more faith, but greater sensitivity to the voice of the Holy Spirit—because His voice creates faith and empowers us to overcome what seems impossible. Revelation which communicates the will of God is responsibility of the Holy Spirit and clarity to hear and receive is our responsibility.

In my own life, I do not move forward in decisions until I hear His voice. The Lord has spoken to me about my wife, my children, homes, vehicles, ministry, and more. You might ask, "You didn't buy a house until you heard His voice?" That's correct. I wanted to be sure I had the grace to step into the right home in the right season. Faith and obedience produce grace, and the same grace that opens the door also sustains what God has given. The grace that helped us step into a home is the same grace that sustains it, including meeting the financial responsibility of paying for it.

But on the flip-side, when I heard from the Lord when and where to buy a house, it required my wife's faith and vision to partner with mine in order to find our miracle home. I was so quick to buy a house that initially seemed right for us, that I was willing to compromise our dreams. But Kristen was persistent and told me to look into building a home within a gated neighborhood. I was reluctant at first, but I came to realize it was the God decision to purchase a lot and build our home. It wasn't until we were in the building process that we both realized that I had forgotten the dream I had about the home years earlier and the home we built looks exactly like the one we put on our vision board. Undeniably, God had His hand in this process all along.

Ephesians 2:8 NIV says, *"For it is by grace you have been saved, through faith—and this is not from yourselves, it is the gift of God."* This is why I spent so much time in the previous chapter distinguishing between following feelings and following the voice of God. If God did not speak to you about where to be planted in a church, whom to marry, what job to take, what business to start, or where to live, you may not have His grace for it. And if you do not have grace for it, you will be ill-equipped for it and will be forced to maintain it through your own strength—resulting in toil and hardship (see Proverbs 10:22).

This is also why God places people in our lives to help us discern His voice. Grace not only opens the door to healing or breakthrough; it sustains life. Living by grace is living a life of rest in Him.

Relationships of the Nine Gifts

1 Corinthians 12:8–9 (NKJV) says, *"For to one is given the word of wisdom through the Spirit, to another the word of knowledge through the same Spirit, to another faith by the same Spirit, to another gifts of healings by the same Spirit, to another the working of miracles, to another prophecy, to another discerning of spirits, to another different kinds of tongues, to another the interpretation of tongues."*

Because every gift of revelation flows from the same Holy Spirit, the gifts are not meant to be isolated from one another. You may sense greater confidence or experience in one gift over another, but the Holy Spirit desires to work through you in all of them. In practice, I have found that when the gifts of the Spirit are in operation, one gift is often for the one ministering, while another is for the person receiving ministry.

For example, we may receive a word of knowledge from the Holy Spirit, but the healing itself is for the other person to receive. Discernment may be sensed by one of our altar team members when someone is in need of emotional healing, or when the Holy Spirit wants to identify what spiritual influences are at work in a person's life. That discernment then places a demand on the gift of prophecy, which can then be released to the recipient for encouragement, direction, or freedom.

Receiving a Word of Knowledge

A Word of Knowledge is supernatural insight given by the Holy Spirit, revealing facts or details we couldn't know naturally, so that faith can build and lives can be transformed with just one word. You can receive a word of knowledge anywhere and at any time. The more I anchor my affection in Jesus, the more frequently I receive words, visions, or impressions concerning others. When God speaks to you personally, He communicates in your language. For example, my wife, Kristen, is a nurse and God often communicates to her in medical terms to make it more relatable to her. But when He speaks to you on behalf of someone else, the message often comes wrapped in *their* language—their emotions, experiences, and frame of reference.

Because of this, some words of knowledge require the participation of the person receiving them to fully understand or apply what God is saying. If the word pertains to healing, assume it is a "now" word. In that moment, the Holy Spirit is priming the pump—releasing grace and supernatural ability for healing right then and there.

Words of knowledge are birthed out of intimacy with God and are initiated by the Holy Spirit when I choose to surrender my will to His. These words remind us that God is meeting us exactly where we are at, proving that He is not distant, but intimately involved in our lives. A word of knowledge is heaven interrupting earth—God revealing what we could never know on our own, not to impress us, but to express His love and closeness to people.

Psalm 116:10 declares, *"I believed, therefore I spoke."* Likewise, 2 Corinthians 4:13 says, *"Since we have the same spirit of faith according to what has been written, 'I believed, and so I spoke,' we also believe, and so we also speak."* The mouth will always speak from what the heart is full of (Matthew 12:34). The words Jesus spoke were Spirit and life (John 6:63). They came from the Holy Spirit, and life was the result for those who trusted in His words.

When we receive a word, we never assume we know who it is for, so we remain tentative and humble in how we release it. If we experience a sensory pain, we do not assume we know the condition by naming it—unless the Holy Spirit clearly reveals the name to us. Instead, we simply describe what the Holy Spirit is showing, no more and no less. Sometimes my wife, the nurse, is able to bring medical clarity to it, but we are cautious to call out an incorrect ailment, so we may give the general area of pain and some *possible* conditions it *could* be.

In a one-on-one setting, we might ask, "Do you have pain in this one particular area ____?" and observe how the person responds. In a small group, we may say, "Does anyone have pain in their knee?" We try not to get caught up in left or right sides. If we sense the pain on the right side, we explain that we could be mirroring someone else's pain and let the audience know that healing is available for either knee.

If someone responds to the word and is open to prayer, we pray for them. If they are hesitant or decline, we do not embarrass them; instead, we gently encourage them. In a church setting, we often remind people that a word of knowledge is a "now" word and encourage them to respond in the moment, because their healing is available for the taking, and we are intentionally building faith in the atmosphere. At times, they may ask to receive prayer later, and that is fine. If someone approaches us after the service, we kindly explain that the goal is to strengthen faith, not unintentionally diminish it... so it's important in the future to grab ahold of those words as they are given.

Ways the Holy Spirit May Communicate a Word of Knowledge

Feeling or Sensory Pain:

You may experience a word of knowledge through physical sensations or emotions—such as a sharp or dull pain in a specific area of your body, a throbbing sensation, an unusual feeling, or even a sudden emotion like fear or panic. It's important to discern whether these sensations are truly from the Holy Spirit and not the result of a condition in your own body. It's recommended that you check your body before going into prayer or worship in order to identify your own ailments prior to seeking out sensory words of knowledge that the Holy Spirit is bringing forth for someone's healing.

When receiving a word of knowledge, immediately write it down and then pursue the Holy Spirit for greater clarity so it can be interpreted as accurately as possible. Often, after the initial sensation, the Lord will speak about what the pain represents or shows an impression regarding the condition.

For example, during a pre-service prayer time, My wife and I both felt a dull pain within the inner thigh. Kristen immediately knew it was due to a blood clot. I asked the Lord what it was, and He said, "It's a blood clot causing the pain." Later, we discovered that our neighbor had a blood clot in her inner thigh that traveled into her lungs. The neighbor told my wife she was having difficulty breathing, and Kristen suspected it was the clot from that word of knowledge, broken loose and traveling into her lungs. She checked her oxygen levels, notified the doctor and rushed her to the emergency room immediately. We believe that word from God played a significant role in saving our dear friend's life.

When sensory pain is involved, we may only feel it for a second or two, and often it disappears as soon as we write it down or acknowledge it. Whenever we receive anything from the Holy Spirit, our response is always to ask, "Lord, tell me more about what You are revealing."

I was recently in pre-service prayer when I felt a sudden sensory pain in my hip. I stayed in that moment and asked the Holy Spirit if there was anything more He wanted to show me. Almost immediately, I received an impression—a clear picture of an elderly woman walking slightly bent over, using a black cane in her right hand.

There were a few people around me at the time, so I shared with them that a woman would come into the service bent over with a hip issue, using a black cane in her right hand. I also told my eldest son that this would happen in the second service, not the first.

When the second service began, an elderly woman walked into the sanctuary bent over, using a black cane in her right hand. She was a regular attendee, but this was the first time she had ever used a cane. Because this was the strongest word of knowledge I had received that day, I released it first to the congregation and invited her to come forward for prayer. When we prayed, she said the pain left her hip immediately. By releasing this strongest word of knowledge first, and seeing healing take place, it activated the faith of the congregation, allowing room for other healings to be received.

Seeing:

You may receive a word of knowledge through mental pictures. These can appear as images of body parts—such as a heart, foot, eye, head, or spine—or as exaggerated conditions, like one leg appearing longer than the other or one eye appearing significantly larger than the other. You might see a person guarding an arm, using a crutch, wearing glasses, walking with a cane, holding a water bottle, or even symbolic images like barbed wire, an auto accident, or an injury.

At times, I see what looks like an X-ray image of a person's body. On one occasion, I gave a word of knowledge about back pain. A teenager came forward to the altar for prayer. Before I prayed, I stepped back and asked the Holy Spirit what was happening in his body. Immediately, I saw a vivid picture of an X-ray showing three vertebrae twisted out of alignment. The image was so clear that I said to him, "You have scoliosis of the spine."

He was stunned and asked how I knew. I told him that I saw it and that it wasn't his entire spine, but a small section in his lower back. He confirmed that this was exactly right—he had been diagnosed in eighth grade, and it had kept him from entering the military.

I prayed for him and told him to sit back down and that Jesus would manifest his healing. The following Sunday, he returned and shared that his spine was now straight. He had grown about an inch and a half over the past week due to the straightening of the spine. And he was later cleared to enlist in the military.

You may also receive a vision as prophetic word for someone, only when God feels the time is right. Our son Aden would often ask me, "Mom, what is God showing you for my future wife?" But God would not reveal anything to me while he was dating his current girlfriend at the time. Then one day, while I was singing during worship, God showed me a vision of Aden, with his future wife and toddler standing up at the altar. However, it was not the girlfriend he had been dating. When I told Aden of what I saw, he confessed that he had just broken up with his girlfriend a couple days prior and didn't know how to tell us. The oppression that had rested on that ungodly relationship had blocked our ability to see beyond it to what God truly has for him.

Reading:

You may receive a word of knowledge by *reading* what appears in your mind. This can look like a word written across a person's chest or back, hovering over their head, displayed on a wall or carpet, or appearing like a headline, sign, or banner. I experience this often in deliverance settings.

On one occasion, a man came forward to the altar who appeared joyful and kind. As he stood in front of me, the Holy Spirit drew my attention to his eyes. At times, the Spirit emphasizes a specific feature by enlarging it in my perception. In this moment, I saw his black pupil in his right eye expand dramatically, and within it, in clear white letters written in cursive, I saw the word **"Anger."**

When he stepped up for prayer, I told him, "You don't need to be angry anymore." He immediately broke down in tears and he asked how I knew. I explained how I had seen it. He shared that anger had been the root of his addiction, the lens in which he views everything through (hence the eye) and in that moment, he received deliverance.

More recently, a woman came to the altar and I saw the word **"REST"** appear in large, bold white letters. In another instance, I saw nearly a hundred words floating above a woman's head. I knew instantly that it represented confusion. Later, I learned she had received many conflicting "prophetic" words that contradicted one another and left her overwhelmed and unsure.

These moments remind me that the Holy Spirit communicates with clarity and purpose, even when the message comes through something as simple as a word seen in the spirit.

An Impression ("Thinking" the Word):

An impression is a knowing that forms in your mind—a sense that the Holy Spirit has communicated something to you about a person or a condition. It is not something you reason out; it simply *arrives* as a mental impression.

At times, I may see a body part and simultaneously receive an impression of what is happening to it. For example, I might suddenly think of a specific condition, such as *ulcerative colitis*, an inflammation of the intestines, without having any natural way of knowing it.

On another occasion at the altar, I saw an image of spinal discs stacked on top of one another, visibly eroding. I asked the Lord what I was seeing, and the phrase *degenerative disc disease* immediately came to mind. When I called it out, a woman raised her hand and began walking toward me for prayer—she had been diagnosed with that exact condition.

Impressions often come quietly and clearly, yet with authority. When recognized and spoken in faith, they become an invitation to partner with what God is already doing.

Speaking:

Sometimes, while talking, praying, or simply standing with someone, unplanned words will come out of your mouth—words connected to a physical condition you had no prior awareness of. These moments are not premeditated; they flow spontaneously. Almost as if you blurt it out uncontrollably.

One night, I walked into a prayer meeting and noticed a woman whose feet had been severely swollen for two weeks. The swelling was so extreme that I honestly did not know how she managed to get her shoes on. As I walked past her, I suddenly pointed at her and said, "You won't leave the same way you came in."

Everyone in the room smiled—but I immediately covered my mouth and thought, *Why did I just say that?* After the initial panic passed, I realized this was a word of knowledge.

I quietly asked the Lord what I should do next, and He said, "Command the capillaries to open." I replied, "That sounds great… but what is a capillary?" There was no further response, so I quickly looked it up on Google and learned that capillaries are the small blood vessels in the body—especially abundant in extremities like the feet.

With confidence in what the Holy Spirit had revealed, I asked everyone to watch what God was about to do. I pointed at the woman's feet and said, "Capillaries, open now, in the name of Jesus!"

She immediately said she felt her feet shift inside her shoes as space was created. When she got into her car, they shifted again, creating even more room. By the next morning, she woke up completely healed.

When thoughts bubble up unexpectedly and are spoken in faith, they can become the very doorway through which God releases healing.

A Dream:

You may receive a word of knowledge through a vivid dream or supernatural vision. In the dream, you might experience a new health issue yourself, see someone else with a specific condition, or hear someone talking about a health problem. These dreams often carry clarity and weight, leaving a strong impression when you wake up.

Dreaming can be a way obtaining a directional or prophetic word. He often speaks to me through dreams to remove much of my ability to interfere or overanalyze; the message is clear, sealed, and difficult to distort. In other words, it prevents my own thoughts from getting in the way. Job 33:15 (NKJV) says, *"In a dream, in a vision of the night, when deep sleep falls upon men, while slumbering on their beds, then He opens the ears of the men, and seals their instruction."* God speaks revelation to our subconscious while we sleep. And like mentioned before, He will speak in a language you can interpret.

Some years back, when I was still nursing in the hospital setting, I had a dream about taking care of a patient that was hooked up to an IV pump in order to stay alive. At the root of the dream, however, I found that the IV pump was not plugged into the electrical outlet, therefore that person was not tapping into the life-force readily available to them—God—for His power to restore that person. John 15:5 (NASB) says, *"I am the vine, you are the branches; he who abides in Me and I in him, he bears much fruit, for apart from Me you can do nothing."* When I woke from this dream, I had the understanding that this person needs to be plugged into the source (through His vine or metaphorical electrical cord) if they want to receive healing. This person was deceived as they were plugged into an inferior source. *"Planted in the house of the Lord, they will flourish in the courts of our God"* (Psalm 92:13).

When waking from a dream that you feel holds powerful meaning, it is crucial to write it down and ask the Lord questions, such as, "Who is this dream for?" "What does this mean?" And allow the Holy Spirit to continue to speak to you. Don't get too hung up on all the details, but focus on the tone, and the key points. A great resource for understanding dreams is *"God's Prophetic Symbolism in Everyday Life"* by Adam F Thompson and Adrian Beale.

Experience It:

Similarly to dreaming, you may receive a word of knowledge through a vivid vision while fully awake. At times, the experience can be so intense that you are not merely observing what is happening—you feel as though you are living it.

I own a restoration company and once visited a job site where a plumber had just installed fixtures in a bathtub. As I walked into the bathroom, I saw him wince in pain. On his wrist was a WWJD bracelet, so I asked what had happened. He told me he had been in a motorcycle accident. In an instant, I found myself standing on a roadway, watching him ride his motorcycle as a car rear-ended him. When I described what I saw, he said that was exactly how the accident occurred.

At that moment, I knew the Holy Spirit was giving me permission to pray for him. I asked if he went to church, and he said, "I'm Catholic." I replied, "That's great—may I pray for your back right now?" He agreed. I asked him to turn around so I could place my hand on his back and then, I prayed a short, simple prayer. As I did, I heard something stretch and snap in his back. Immediately, I knew that he had been healed.

I asked him to bend over and test his back. He did—and said the pain was completely gone. When he turned back around, he was crying and looking at his arms. He asked, "What is this all over my body?" I smiled and said, "My friend, that is the Holy Spirit."

Smell:

Smell is not as common a method to receive words of knowledge. It is often known as a "spiritual scent" that holds symbolic meaning, without natural explanation. At times, I have sensed distinct fragrances on people—such as flowers or a sweet aroma—that carry a deep sense of peace, comfort or God's presence. Second Corinthians 2:14–15 describes us as the *"aroma of Christ."* And in Psalm 141:2, *"Your prayers rise like incense."*

On the other hand, I have also detected smells like smoke, rotten eggs, or sulfur on individuals or in certain homes, which I often associate with demonic influence. Sulfur can also represent fear, shame past trauma, illness. But smoke can also represent fire, which biblically, is a refining or purification process that is taking place as that person is going through transformation. In Malachi 3 it states, *"He will sit as a refiner and purifier of silver."* Before anything else, discernment needs to come first, to rule out any real fire, gas leak or environmental reason for the smell.

Emotions:

Words of knowledge can also be received regarding a person's emotional state. Just as words of knowledge for physical healing often manifest as sensory or bodily pain, emotional words of knowledge operate in a similar way—you may actually feel what the other person is experiencing emotionally.

One time, my wife's cousin and her boyfriend were walking up our driveway from about a hundred feet away as they were coming from another state to spend the weekend with us. I had never met the boyfriend before, yet as soon as I saw him I told my wife, "He has issues with anger." She asked how I knew, and I explained that I could feel it, especially since anger is not something I personally struggle with. Often, demonic assignments operating in a person's life can be projected outward, making them easy to discern if you are sensitive to the Spirit. Over that weekend, I witnessed repeated fits of rage from the man, confirming what had been revealed. We were able to utilize this knowledge to warn her cousin and reveal the red flags that the Holy Spirit showed me in that first instance.

Practical Insights

Words of knowledge are spontaneous and often arrive quickly. I once heard Bill Johnson share that before entering a grocery store, he would pause and intentionally focus on the Holy Spirit. As he walked through the store, he would sense the atmosphere shift—and the people around him would feel it as well. I shop at Costco frequently and do the same thing before I walk inside. As I shift my focus to the Holy Spirit, I often receive words of knowledge for people as I pass them.

When we gather for pre-service prayer on Sunday mornings with the altar team, I remind them that this is no difference than a normal day at Costco. In other words, this is what we were created to do. Words of knowledge are an expression of the Father's love to His children. I don't assume that I have more mercy for God's children than He does. He desires to heal far more than we desire to see people healed, so we don't need to beg Him to do what is already in His heart.

During service or worship, we have the altar team sit near the front and write down their words of knowledge to share at the altar with the strongest words first. While worship continues, we pray and discern which words of knowledge are to be released. We then prioritize them from strongest to weakest, because words of knowledge are meant to build faith, and accuracy and clarity matter. The more specific and consistent the words are, the more faith they produce.

We typically minister words of knowledge immediately after worship, while the focus is still on Jesus. One of the most effective ways to release words of knowledge is by first charging the atmosphere with testimonies of healing and deliverance. We may share a story of Jesus healing in Scripture or a recent testimony from our church. The testimony of Jesus releases prophetic power for healing and deliverance into the atmosphere.

Revelation 19:10 says, *"Worship God. For the testimony of Jesus is the spirit of prophecy."* Worship gives us access to what Jesus owns. The Hebrew word for testimony, *uwd*, means "to repeat" or "to do again." Prophecy speaks and creates what will be. When a testimony is released, a prophetic anointing fills the room, and what Jesus did for one person, He desires to do again for another.

When releasing words of knowledge, I usually begin with the ones the Lord has personally given me, then I look for repetition among the words written down by the altar team. If the same condition appears two or three times, it moves to the top of the list. I start with the words I feel most confident about, then move to those that carry a question mark. Remember, faith is also spelled R-I-S-K. Don't become satisfied with only one way of operating—continue to place a demand on God to grow in areas where you feel less confident.

Another approach is to have the altar lead release their words of knowledge and then invite the rest of altar team forward to release theirs. In this tactic, we want the congregation to clearly see who received which word. If someone receives a general prayer and does not experience immediate improvement, they can then receive direct prayer from the person who originally received the word. If God entrusted that word to them, He has also given them the grace to minister healing through it.

I have seen many people healed of head trauma. In fact, I have personally prayed for three individuals with brain tumors that completely disappeared. When head trauma comes up, I don't always need a word of knowledge to pursue healing—I already carry faith to see the Holy Spirit move, since He has already provided grace in that area.

You might wonder about those who need healing but did not receive a word of knowledge. Words of knowledge create faith; they are the spark that ignites the fire. When someone responds to a word of knowledge, receives healing, and testifies to that healing, the atmosphere becomes charged with faith. You can feel the increase in the room. It is often in that moment that I begin to pursue healing for those who did not initially receive a specific word of knowledge.

Do Whatever He Tells You To Do

In John 2, Jesus and His disciples attended a wedding in Cana of Galilee where the wine ran out. Mary already had a deep history with God and understood that grace empowers what it commands. Because of this, she recognized that where there is a need, there is also a gift—and if Jesus spoke a word, the Holy Spirit would bring it to pass. That is why Mary told the servants in John 2:5, *"Do whatever He tells you."* Don't overthink it or try to rationalize it—simply obey, and you will see the grace of God manifest.

We must learn to stay in our lane, obedient, and do whatever the Holy Spirit instructs us to do. We are not called to reduce the revelation of God's Word to the limits of our understanding, but to trust in Him and not lean on our own understanding (Proverbs 3:5).

Receiving a word of knowledge for someone is much like Jesus calling out to Blind Bartimaeus in Mark 10:46–52. Do you think Jesus would call someone forward and then withhold what He desires to do? When Jesus calls a person, it is their appointed time for healing or a miracle.

After revealing to His disciples that He would go to the cross, Jesus spoke about sending the Holy Spirit, because He did not want His followers to be ill-equipped. John 16:13–14 (ESV) says, *"When the Spirit of truth comes, He will guide you into all the truth, for He will not speak on His own authority, but whatever He hears He will speak, and He will declare to you the things that are to come. He will glorify Me, for He will take what is Mine and declare it to you."*

When the Holy Spirit speaks to you, the words you hear originate with Jesus. Words of knowledge build faith for healing and deliverance because they testify that Jesus Himself is calling to the person—and that their sudden break is at hand. When you receive and declare a word of knowledge, it is as though Jesus is standing beside you, releasing the same decree.

Chapter 5 - Prophecy

"For you can all prophesy one by one, so that all may learn and all may be encouraged" (1 Corinthians 14:31). Paul also exhorts us to *"follow the way of love and eagerly desire gifts of the Spirit, especially prophecy"* (1 Corinthians 14:1). In saying this, Paul makes it clear that all believers may prophesy, because His sheep hear His voice.

Larry Randolph once said, "To possess a gift without purpose is to waste the gift that has been given. If there is a prophetic gift or ministry, there is a prophetic purpose." The Holy Spirit manifests gifts in response to need. The level of anointing in a service is directly connected to the needs of the people present. If there is a need around you, know that the Holy Spirit is already there and will equip you to meet it. Jesus illustrated this in the parable of the man who went to borrow three loaves of bread to meet a friend's need (Luke 11:5–13). If you ask God for bread on behalf of someone else, will He give you a stone?

Prophecy is God speaking through people to bring divine encouragement. At its core, it is simply hearing from God and speaking what you hear in order to strengthen, comfort, or encourage someone. To move prophetically, you must believe that God not only wants to speak, but that He desires to speak in and through you. As 1 Corinthians 14:3 (NIV) says, *"The one who prophesies speaks to people for their strengthening, encouraging and comfort."*

Love is the motive behind every spiritual gift. If love is not your motive, neither you nor your gift will be received (1 Corinthians 13:1). Words are not easily received without a foundation of trust, and trust is built through love. The Mirror Translation of 1 Corinthians 13:7 says, *"Love is a fortress where everyone feels protected rather than exposed."* This places a strong emphasis on the heart behind the gift.

Prophecy has three key components. The first is revelation, which unveils something hidden. The second is interpretation, which clarifies what the Holy Spirit is saying. The third is application, or administration, which determines how and when the word is to be ministered. Some words are meant to be released immediately, while others are given for intercession and are not yet meant to be shared. A word released outside of God's timing can feel like condemnation and cause harm rather than encouragement. Remember, the Holy Spirit speaks to you in your language, but He often speaks through you in someone else's language. What carries meaning for you may carry a different meaning for them.

"Speaking in tongues builds up the individual, while prophecy builds up the church" (1 Corinthians 14:4). Words of knowledge are just as vital in prophecy as they are in healing. I once spoke with a young woman who told me she was in a crusade where someone prayed over her and declared she was called to Mexico. I asked her, "Did the person begin with a word of knowledge about you?" She said "No." And I responded, "Words without God are just words." A word of knowledge brings credibility to both prophecy and healing. When I prophesy over someone I do not know, the Holy Spirit will often give me a word of knowledge first to confirm that what follows is truly from Him. When there is an established trust relationship, I will often share what the Holy Spirit is saying only when I sense release to do so.

Two Prophetic Streams

"Now the acts of King David, from first to last, are recorded in the book of Samuel the seer (ra'ah), in the book of Nathan the prophet (nabiy'), and in the book of Gad the seer (chozeh)" (1 Chronicles 29:29). This passage reveals distinct prophetic expressions that function differently, yet work together to communicate the heart and mind of God.

The **nabiy' prophet** operates in spontaneity and is activated by faith, with an emphasis on hearing and speaking. The word *nabiy'* means "to flow forth like a river" or "to bubble up like a fountain." Because of how the *nabiy'* prophet receives from the Holy Spirit, they can often release what they hear immediately. Their delivery is usually faster than that of a seer, as they tend to move straight to the core of an issue without extensive processing.

In contrast, the **ra'ah** or **chozeh seer** is primarily visual and can only hear as much as they see. *Ra'ah* means "to see, to gaze, to look upon, or to perceive." *Chozeh* literally means "a beholder in vision," and can also be translated as "gazer" or "stargazer." *Chozeh* describes who they are, while *ra'ah* describes how they function. Seers often receive revelation ahead of time and release it later, as their process involves interpreting what the Holy Spirit is revealing through images, impressions, or visions.

One of our spiritual fathers is a *nabiy'* prophet. As I served him over the years while he ministered prophetically, I would often think, *He is so much smarter than me*, because of the speed and clarity with which he flowed. Seers, however, are deeply dependent on the presence of God and can only share what they see, which naturally results in a *slower pace*. They are interpreting visual revelation and translating it into words. Unlike the spontaneous nature of the *nabiy'* prophet, seers are often given information in advance so it can be discerned, interpreted, and applied accurately.

Every Sunday, we open the altar to minister prophetically and pray for the sick. During worship one Sunday, I noticed a man walk past me wearing black dress shoes. After he passed, the image of that black shoe remained before me, and suddenly I saw a drill driving a screw into a man's heel. The image was unusual enough that I had to pause and pursue it. I call moments like this "burning bush" encounters—revelation that demands further inquiry. I became anxious because there was only one or two songs left before opening the altar and I needed clarity because the Holy Spirit just spoke. As I asked the Holy Spirit what it meant, the word *betrayal* came strongly to my spirit. This was not an individual word, but a corporate one. The screw represented an attachment, and the wounded heel symbolized betrayal—yet also pointed to victory on the other side of forgiveness and deliverance (Genesis 3:15). When I opened the altar and released the word, several people came forward to receive freedom from wounds that had held them captive.

Like praying in tongues, the *nabiy'* prophetic flow is activated by faith. When you begin praying in tongues, the Holy Spirit eventually takes over. The *nabiy'* prophetic works the same way. Just as with journaling, you may begin by praying in tongues, declaring Scripture, or confessing a promise over someone's life, and suddenly words begin to flow. You remain aware of what you are saying, but you are yielding your mouth to the Holy Spirit and allowing Him to speak.

"I will raise up for them a Prophet [nabiy'] like you from among their brethren, and will put My words in His mouth, and He shall speak to them all that I command Him" (Deuteronomy 18:18).

The delivery of prophets and seers differs. Seers can move prophetically, but prophets do not function as seers. Both may begin differently and minister differently yet often arrive at the same conclusion. Unlike seers, *nabiy'* prophets require little preparation; words automatically rise up and flow out. They may start with a single word impressed on their heart, and the rest follows naturally. A *nabiy'* prophet typically operates through hearing and vocalization, but does not move in visionary revelation the way a seer does. A *chozeh* seer may not immediately pinpoint the issue, but will arrive there through discernment and interpretation of the vision. A *chozeh* seer may see a single word or image and then step into a *nabiy'* flow, sharing in that same grace—but a *nabiy'* prophet cannot step into the revelatory grace of a seer. Both expressions are different, and both are essential.

Because my wife and I are seers, we often begin with a vision or impression (and in her case, dreams). We may share what we see, and then the *nabiy'* prophetic begins to flow from that place. One Sunday, as I opened the altar, I noticed a young mother standing toward the back of the room. Her face stood out among the crowd, and I could see the emotional weight she was carrying. I sensed the Lord wanted to speak to her, but I did not know what to say. I knew that if I opened my mouth in faith, the Holy Spirit would supply the words. I began with what I knew and quoted Matthew 11:28, telling her, *"The Lord sees the burden you are carrying and wants you to give it to Him."* What came next surprised me. I said, "You don't need more education—you need the anointing." As soon as I said it, I saw the Holy Spirit come upon her. I laid hands on her, and she fell under the power of God. After the service, her mother approached me and asked, "Did you know what you said?" I told her no. She explained that her daughter was at a crossroads with returning to school. This was more about identity than direction. The word was not about returning to school but her attitude towards school as she felt it was the accreditation she needed for identity when God has already approved of her as His child.

On another occasion, a friend began talking to me about reconnecting with her father after many years. Immediately, I saw an impression of a father from a reality television show whose story mirrored what she was describing. In that show, the father had given his daughter up for adoption and later reconnected with her after she became successful—only to approach her with a financial agenda. As my friend spoke, I recognized the purpose of the impression and gently cautioned her that her father's motives might not be pure. I told her he might see her lifestyle and attempt to reinsert himself into her life for financial reasons. Sadly, that word later proved to be accurate.

Priming the Pump

I have heard some leaders teach that walking in signs and wonders requires an intense focus on gaining more faith. I disagree. The problem with this approach is that it shifts the focus back onto you and often makes the walk of signs and wonders feel unattainable. Jesus desires to heal far more than we desire to see people healed. Scripture makes it clear that faith is created by hearing the voice of God (Romans 10:17). Your identity must be rooted in the belief that the Holy Spirit wants to speak to you and use you as His redemptive solution to someone else's need. Jesus said He could do nothing on His own, but only what He saw the Father doing, because the Father loves the Son and shows Him everything He does (John 5:19–20).

To create faith for healing, the Holy Spirit often "primes the pump" by showing you what He is already doing. He may initiate it through a word, an impression, a vision, a dream, or a person who suddenly stands out in a crowd. Something around you may catch your attention because it feels out of place, or a particular feature on a person may appear exaggerated, drawing emphasis to an area the Lord wants to heal. These moments are what we had mentioned earlier as "burning bush" moments—unusual encounters that stand out and require pursuit if you truly want to hear what God is saying.

Priming the pump is taking an initial action to encourage a greater result. You put something in first so more can flow out later. The phrase comes from the process of priming an old water pump, where a small amount of water is poured in to expel air and create suction so the pump can function properly. In other words, you add a little so that much more can come.

When our heart's affection is anchored in Jesus, we find that this is when the Holy Spirit loves to speak. He pours from the abundance of the pump by giving us something to respond to. In healing, when we shift our focus to Jesus in worship or prayer, the Holy Spirit will often initiate communication through something like sensory pain to capture my attention. We may feel a sudden flash of pain or a dull ache in an area of our body where we have no history of injury. This sensation may last only a few seconds, until we acknowledge the Holy Spirit. When we do, we ask Him what He is showing us and whether there is anything more we need to know. He may, then, provide additional details—such as an internal "x-ray," the name of a condition, insight into how an injury occurred, or simply leave it at the sensory pain. Learning to recognize and respond to these promptings takes practice.

In prophecy, a person's face may suddenly flash before you, or you may receive an impression, a vision, or even a dream. Remember, it is the Holy Spirit who brings these things "suddenly." Often, He gives only one piece of the puzzle—but it is the exact piece needed to connect with that person. Press into it in order to gain more knowledge in that prophetic word. At times, when we are in a group or a church setting, we will ask the Holy Spirit who He wants to encourage and then, we slowly scan the room. Frequently, one individual or face will stand out among the crowd. This is what priming the pump can look like, and usually that is all you are given until you invite the person forward for prayer.

When I open my mouth, I may begin by speaking a Scripture, trusting that the Holy Spirit will step in and release His word through me. When I am operating in the *Nabiy'* prophetic flow, I often find myself both speaking and listening at the same time—almost as an observer. At times, I am just as surprised by what comes out of my mouth as the person receiving the word.

Scripture tells us, *"Yet God has made everything beautiful for its own time. He has planted eternity in the human heart, but even so, people cannot see the whole scope of God's work from beginning to end"* (Ecclesiastes 3:11 NLT). When the Holy Spirit gives you a word of knowledge for someone, understand that He has already been at work in their heart. He has been stirring within them long before you ever spoke. Your word is an invitation to participate in what God is already doing and to bring confirmation to something they may already sense but not fully understand. Through the prophetic, you help confirm the scope of God's work within them and bring it into completion.

For example, during the holidays I was spending time with my extended family, along with my wife, Kristen, and our kids. As I looked at my sister, I saw bold white letters across her chest that read, "Kristen...Clinic." It was just one word, but I immediately knew she was contemplating her next step as a nurse, even though she may not have realized that the stirring in her heart was from God. How did I know? A prophetic word in the New Testament is confirmation to what the Lord is already speaking to them. If I get a word for someone, I know the Holy Spirit already spoke to them about it even though they may not have recognized it was from God. To them, they could have received a word or a burden for the subject matter and God desires to help them receive it. When I saw this, I asked her if she was at a crossroads of decision regarding her professional career. She said she was. She was contemplating retiring as a nurse or doing something else. I simply encouraged her to talk with my wife and consider working with her in a clinic setting, believing that God had more for the both of them. In that moment, I was there to help nudge them in the right direction. Eternal words from God leave an imprint on a person's heart—one that is not easily dismissed.

Maturity

When you communicate God's heart in love, your message will almost always be received by the person you are ministering to. Many times, I receive words for people I already have a relationship with, and in those cases I may not need a word of knowledge at all. If the person is spiritually mature, I can share the wisdom and encourage them to pray into it so they can receive further insight from the Holy Spirit. However, the less mature someone is, the more guidance they will need. Just as babies cannot raise themselves, I cannot expect a spiritually immature person to "pray about it" and receive revelation that is beyond their current level of faith.

Recently, I was speaking with someone the Lord highlighted to me as a "toddler" in the prophetic. In other words, they were beginning to hear God's voice but believed they were more mature than they actually were at the time. The Lord showed me in an open vision what was going to happen in the near future. Instead of releasing the word, I held onto it and simply encouraged them to pray about a certain area, sensing that the Lord was calling them to prepare for what was ahead. I did this because I wanted them to choose obedience from a pure heart and did not want to manipulate them in any way.

However, when it became clear that they were not hearing from God and were spiritually heading toward a cliff, I went back to the Lord and said, "I repent as I need to tell them what is coming." The Lord responded clearly, "I never told you *not* to tell them." He continued, "They are toddlers, and this word is far beyond their level of faith. They would never receive this on their own. You must treat them like a toddler and be direct in your communication."

Orphans, babies, and/or toddlers in Christ cannot yet eat solid food; they need mature believers to help them recognize the voice of God and discern between good and evil, or between the flesh and the Spirit. It is through constant use or obedience that they will mature in their discernment (Hebrews 5:14). Because of this, I have found that understanding a person's level of spiritual maturity is essential to effective communication with God. Their faith has limits at each stage of growth, and those limits must be recognized and respected in order to minister to them wisely and lovingly.

There are five stages of maturity starting with:

1. Orphans (see John 14:18; James 1:27)

Everyone comes into the church as an orphan. If a person chooses not to be fathered or discipled, they can remain in this stage indefinitely. This person can feel a sense of abandonment or lack of belonging. They struggle to believe they are worthy of love, leaving them thinking they are unsupported and tend to resist authority, as they become self-reliant.

2. Babies (see Luke 1:41; 2:12)

A baby is someone who has recently given their life to Christ and is a spiritual infant. Babies require milk, not solid food (1 Corinthians 3:2; Hebrews 5:12–14). They have a lot to learn from God and the church to help shape and mold their identity in Christ.

3. Toddlers (see 1 Corinthians 3:1)

Toddlers still need milk rather than meat. They begin to recognize that they are gifted and often try to move beyond their level of maturity, authority, or responsibility. They now have faith, but may press limits beyond that level of faith. They may complain, become jealous, or desire to be seen as adults (gifted in talents) before they are ready—sometimes making a mess along the way.

4. Children (see Matthew 18:2–4; Luke 2:40)

Those who humble themselves and become like children in the Kingdom are trained by the Holy Spirit to be great in the Kingdom. Children listen to their Father, remain teachable, and are able to forgive the mistakes of others.

5. Sons and Daughters (see John 8:35)

Sons and daughters are born into or adopted into the family and share the nature of their Father. They are mature, whole, and complete because they are committed to the process of growth and transformation (Matthew 5:48; Ephesians 4:13; and James 1:4). Hebrews 5:14 (BSB) says, *"But solid food is for the mature, who by constant use have trained their senses to distinguish good from evil."*

Economic Prophets

If you are called to any level of ministry, someone will have to fund the vision. The same grace I operate in prophetically is the same grace I depend on in business. I have been self-employed for nearly thirty years; June 17, 1997 was my last day working for someone else. While I was employed at a grocery store, the Lord spoke to me and said, "Your job cannot pay for the call that I've placed on your life."

Walking away from a steady paycheck terrified me because of the faith it required. Still, I was more afraid of disobedience than of being poor. The real question is this: **What is God telling you to leave?** Jesus said that whatever we leave for His sake, He will return a hundredfold in this life (Mark 10:29–30).

"Believe in the Lord your God, and you will be established; believe His prophets, and you will prosper [tsalach]" (2 Chronicles 20:20). *Tsalach* means to break out on every side and to prosper. One of the purposes of the prophetic is to break people out of whatever box is restraining them so they can step into God's provision and purpose. The prophetic is meant for breakout and increase.

On May 5, 2022, I had a vivid dream in which about twenty witches entered a Christian town and began moving in and out of businesses owned by believers. Across the street, I saw the head witch and knew I was functioning as a watchman for the town. When she realized I recognized her, she called out to the others, and they quickly retreated across a river and into the mountains. I was shown that the place they fled to had once been occupied by Christians but had been forfeited to the enemy and turned into a demonic stronghold.

We pursued them to their town and found ourselves standing among the witches, including their leader. The believers came with me began going through their shops, while I stood in the center of town with the head witch and the others. As the head witch approached me, I commanded the demons to leave her, and they did. When the rest of the witches saw this, they ran through the streets in a panic shouting, "The children of God are coming, and they are not going to stop!" When I woke up, I prophesied what I had seen. Even the demonic response confirmed the plan of God for His people.

Demonic strongholds are going to be breached, and they will fall. God will save what once seemed unsalvageable. To set this in motion, a prophetic voice is required to create a breach in the enemy's camp. God is raising up a people who will not only minister in the church, but who will also carry His authority and provision into the marketplace.

Jesus said, *"When a strong man, fully armed, guards his own house, his possessions are secure. But when someone stronger attacks and overpowers him, he takes away the armor in which the man trusted and divides up his plunder"* (Luke 11:21–22).

Breaching Strongholds

To further illustrate this, I was a combat veteran and served six years in the Marine Corps as an infantryman. Much of my time was spent training in the field. One tactic we used to dismantle enemy defense or stronghold was known as a *push-pull offense.* When an enemy maintained a 360-degree defensive position, we would probe their lines to identify a weakness in their perimeter.

Once that weak point was located, we would create confusion through coordinated fire missions and then exploit the opening by rapidly breaching the defense and funneling large numbers of troops through that single point. We had to do this quickly as the place of the breach will always be the place where fire is concentrated. After the breach, the enemy could no longer turn their weapons inward and fire without destroying themselves and are forced to surrender. Focusing all of our firepower and manpower on a single weakness allowed us to not only break through the enemy's defense but to pull everyone through who came up behind us.

It was through this dream that I believe the Holy Spirit revealed that He will save the unsavable and that which has been under demonic control which is the media, art, entertainment and even business will shift back to the children of God if we will position ourselves and see what the Holy Spirit would say to us. The manna the children of God ate yesterday will not nourish us today.

I believe this dream also revealed that God is raising up ministers in the marketplace. If God is going to do a new thing in you, you will receive a hundred-blessing in this age and persecutions (Mark 10:30). Persecution will come as it often arises when God calls you to create something new and many are unable to let go of the old. Because of this, you cannot afford to have your mouth bought. Many prophetic people are in fear of saying or doing certain things for fear of losing followers or their paycheck from the ministry that employs them.

Remember, even Jesus offended and said, *"blessed is the one who is not offended by me* (Luke 7:23). I know many highly gifted ministers who struggle financially due to religious mindsets that demonize money and its use. They are often taught that the answer is simply to return to the church and take up more offerings, when God is fully capable of releasing wisdom, strategy, and provision to fund the vision He has given you. Right now, you may be doing ok financially. But, what happens when God puts the burden of a nation on you (Psalm 2:8, Matthew 28:19)? The poor cannot help the poor, and you cannot give that which you do not possess.

I have often heard ministers quote Revelation 1:6, which says that He *"has made us kings and priests to His God and Father."* I once heard Bill Johnson say, "Rule with the heart of a servant, and serve with the heart of a king." These positions may have been separate roles in the past, but I believe kings and priests are one unified calling in the NT by the Holy Spirit. When we attempt to divide them, we subtly imply that one is meant to prosper without spiritual power, while the other is meant to serve in ministry without provision. In God's design, authority and humility, provision and devotion, flow together as a single calling.

When you believe a lie, you empower the liar and unintentionally mute the voice of the Holy Spirit when He speaks about increase. Scripture never says money is evil; it says the **love** of money is the root of all kinds of evil (1 Timothy 6:10). Jesus also taught that we cannot serve both God and mammon (Matthew 6:24). Mammon is a spirit that entices believers to place their trust in wealth rather than in God, which ultimately becomes a form of idolatry.

Many believers remain in a financial struggle not because of a blatant lie, but because of an *almost truth*. Whenever the Lord gives me a vision that is larger than my own capacity, I ask Him how He intends to fund what He has revealed. He consistently responds by releasing wisdom and strategy to support what He has initiated, or he has put it on the hearts of people to support it (Genesis 22:8). Regardless, the burden is not yours to carry but the Lord's.

Creating Something Out of Nothing

In 2 Kings 4:1–7, we read about a widow who had lost her husband and was facing a creditor who intended to take her two sons as slaves. When Elisha asked her what she had in her house, she replied, "Nothing at all—except a jar of oil." Elisha instructed her to borrow as many empty vessels as possible, and as she obeyed, God filled every vessel with oil until there were no more left. God literally created an economy out of something as insignificant as a single jar of oil. The proceeds from her obedience provided for her and her sons for the rest of their lives. This is generational provision. It reveals God's heart toward those who commit themselves to His call and His purposes. The Spirit of God desires to continually pour wisdom and revelation into His children so they can become an untapped resource to a dying world.

"Hope deferred makes the heart sick, but a desire fulfilled is a tree of life" (Proverbs 13:12). A sudden good break can turn everything around. *Sudden* means quickly and without warning—happening all at once and unexpectedly. David experienced this when he defeated the Philistines at Baal Perazim, declaring, *"The Lord has broken through my enemies before me, like a breakthrough of water"* (2 Samuel 5:20). *Unrelenting disappointment makes you heartsick, but a sudden good break can turn life around"* (Proverbs 13:12 Msg). Our God is a God of breakthrough.

Scripture speaks of the sons of Issachar as men who *"understood the times and knew what Israel ought to do"* (1 Chronicles 12:32). In the same way, the Lord may speak to you about creating or acquiring a business to fund the vision He has given you. I believe God desires His people to be recession-proof. Being recession-proof, to me, means stewarding a business or industry that continues to function and provide during economic downturns. Ultimately, the strength of your economy is determined by the "government" you choose to connect it to.

For nearly thirty years, the Lord has spoken to me about economic shifts well in advance so there would be time to prepare. Joseph did this with Pharaoh. It was not enough for Joseph to merely receive revelation about a coming famine; he also received the wisdom to respond to it. Revelation and wisdom go hand in hand (Ephesians 1:17). Without wisdom, revelation is incomplete—it reveals a problem without providing a solution. When revelation comes, wisdom soon follows so you understand your role in what God has revealed. God never reveals a problem without also providing the grace and tools needed to address it. Wisdom is freely given, but revelation and the responsibility that accompanies it will cost you something (James 1:5).

The Lord has shown me future economic failures or "shakings" in certain regions and revealed that we are in a season of preparation, much like the days of Noah building the ark. When people dismiss a word from God and attempt to prepare only once the flood has begun, they become victims of what could have been avoided. Psalm 82:5 says, *"They know nothing, they understand nothing. They walk about in darkness; all the foundations of the earth are shaken."* What shakes the world and moves it into darkness is not meant to shake God's people but it will if we do not pursue the face of Jesus, recognize His voice and move when He tells us to move.

1 Corinthians 14:1 exhorts us to eagerly desire spiritual gifts, especially prophecy. If we want to walk in the prophetic, we must be intentional about cultivating it. Jeremiah 23:22 says, *"If they had stood before Me and listened to Me, they would have spoken My words."* This is not a rebuke but a promise. Before we can speak God's word to others, we must first stand before Him and learn to listen.

When young Samuel struggled to recognize the voice of God, Eli instructed him to respond, *"Speak, Lord, for your servant is listening."* God used Eli to help Samuel discern His voice. In the same way, God places prophetic people in our lives to strengthen areas where we are still growing (Ephesians 4:11–12). Our personal responsibility to hear God's voice does not eliminate the need for prophets, nor does the presence of prophets eliminate our need to hear God for ourselves. If God only spoke to one person, there would be no need for the body of Christ.

Things to Consider

"But the one who prophesies speaks to people for their strengthening, encouragement, and comfort" (1 Corinthians 14:3). The motive behind every spiritual gift must be love, because love is what builds people up. Without love, neither we nor our gifts will be received. With that foundation in mind, here are several important principles to consider:

Be teachable:

Matthew 5:5 says, *"Blessed are the meek, for they shall inherit the earth."* The Greek word for meekness is *"praus"* which means strength exercised under God's control. Meekness speaks to being teachable and to the proper use of God's authority. Those who remain teachable are the ones who inherit what God has promised.

Understand your level of authority:

You do not have authority where you have no responsibility. If you do not carry responsibility within a congregation, you do not carry authority there. Authority is also shaped by submission to spiritual fathers and leadership. Without accountability or covering, prophetic gifting can be misused—what the church has often referred to as "parking lot prophets."

Operate at your level of faith:

God will use you right where you are. Be honest and transparent with people about what you received and how you received it. If the Holy Spirit spoke to you, say what He said. If you saw something, share what you saw. If you only received part of it, that is okay. The person receiving the word may already recognize what God is revealing and can help bring clarity to it.

Check your spiritual lenses:

Ananias initially resisted God's instruction because of what he had heard about Saul (Acts 9:13–14). Discernment often reveals what is wrong with a person or situation, but many stop there and never ask the Holy Spirit what He intends to do about it. Always ask questions. I once saw a man in a grocery store parking lot with smoke coming from his car because he was smoking marijuana. I drove away in judgment, but the Lord immediately said to me, "He is doing the best he can to battle his anxiety." My heart sank, and I repented. Discernment without compassion will limit your influence.

Walk in humility:

We are here to serve. Asking permission before speaking is "prophetic etiquette" It honors the person and allows them to remain in control. Timing matters. Even the right word, delivered at the wrong time, can be counter-productive.

Value accuracy:

Accurate prophetic words confirm what God has already been speaking to someone. Prophecy should not shock the recipient but encourage them by affirming that they are hearing God clearly. In Acts 9:10–18, God sent Ananias to Saul with a very specific assignment. Saul had already encountered God on the road to Damascus, and Ananias simply played his part in what God was already doing. If you have a word for someone, trust that God is already stirring their heart in that area. Many times, I receive a word for someone only to later receive a call asking prayer for the very thing the Lord had already shown me.

Handle directional prophecy with care:

Directional prophecies can be dangerous if they are given out of season or without clear confirmation. This is a caution both for those who give and those who receive such words. Seek confirmation from spiritual leaders, because wisdom is found in a multitude of counselors and every matter is established by two or three witnesses (Proverbs 11:14; 15:22; 24:6; 2 Corinthians 13:2). When two or three trusted voices speak the same word, it is something you should not ignore.

Honor: (see Matthew 10:41 NLT)

One of the quickest ways to grow in the gifts of revelation is through a heart of honor. Honor is an investment that gives you access to a prophet, a righteous person, and the grace that rests on their life. When you receive a prophet or a righteous person, you are ultimately receiving the One who sent them—Jesus Himself.

Honor given from a prophet is the extension of access: an open hand that makes available what they carry. Honor received is being so aware of the value offered that you take what belongs to another and make it your own. This requires listening, embracing, and stewarding the benefit of something you may not have labored for yourself.

On the other hand, dishonor cuts off access to the man or woman of God and their gift. When we dishonor a prophet, a righteous person, or even our parents, we forfeit access to the grace and gift connected to their lives (see Exodus 20:12; John 8:49; Mark 6:4). Jesus said, *"A prophet is honored everywhere except in his own hometown and among his own family"* (Matthew 13:57–58). Because of dishonor, few miracles were done there. Restoration requires repentance—not only a change of heart, but a change in behavior that reestablishes God's standard of righteousness in a believer's life.

Returning Honor:

Before God restored Israel through the tithe, He had to take them through the process of purification in order for them '*to present to the Lord offerings in righteousness*" (Malachi 3:2-3). You cannot resist the refinery. If you do, you will give with a wrong heart or motive (2 Corinthians 9:7) and fail to see into the windows of Heaven and what God has in store for you. In Malachi 3:7, God says, *"Return to me, and I will return to you."* The question Israel asked was, *"How do we return?"* God's answer was, *"In tithes and offerings."* To restore a relationship of honor, Israel had to be refined to make an investment in righteousness. The Hebrew word for "return" is *shub*, which means to return home, recover, be rescued, and be delivered. It also implies recompense—restoring what was once given and then lost. Honor restores access.

God's Will vs. Your Will:

There is the perfect will of God, the permissive will of God, and your will. The perfect will of God is His original intention and highest purpose for your life. Romans 12:2 teaches that as you renew your mind, you will be able to discern and prove God's good, acceptable, and perfect will.

For example, 1 Timothy 2:4 says it is God's desire that all be saved—yet not all are. God's permissive will allows human choice and even mistakes, but through repentance, He works to restore His perfect will. A clear example is Israel asking God to speak through Moses rather than directly to them because His voice frightened them (Exodus 20:19). What was lost there was later restored through Christ, as Jesus said, *"My sheep hear My voice"* (John 10:27).

Your will carries real weight. God will always place two trees in the garden of your heart and allow you to choose. You can prophesy accurately over someone's potential all day long, but the responsibility to choose rests entirely with the person receiving that word. My prayer is that people would choose God's perfect—or at least His permissive—will over their own, because that choice determines whether they live in God's superior design or an inferior version of their calling.

You Are Qualified:

Every believer can prophesy. If you can pray in the Spirit, then you can prophesy. You are qualified, not because of your title, years of experience in the ministry, or maturity level, but because the Spirit of God already dwells within you. Every believer has access to the voice of God, if willing to listen. Prophecy is not about perfection. It is about availability. God is not looking for experts—He is looking for willing vessels.

Chapter 6 - Ministering Healing

Healing the sick was a central and inseparable part of Jesus' ministry. Throughout the Gospels, whenever His work is summarized, healing is consistently mentioned alongside teaching and preaching.

Matthew 4:23 states, *"Jesus went throughout all Galilee, teaching in their synagogues, preaching the gospel of the Kingdom, and healing every disease and every sickness among the people."* Healing was not an occasional act—it was a defining expression of the Kingdom of God in action.

Healing was also included in Jesus' assignment to the twelve disciples. Matthew 10:1, 5, 7–8 tells us that He gave them authority over unclean spirits and power to heal every kind of sickness and disease. He sent them out with this command: *"As you go, preach, saying, 'The kingdom of heaven is at hand. Heal the sick, cleanse the lepers, raise the dead, cast out demons. Freely you have received; freely give.'"*

This mandate did not stop with the twelve. Jesus extended it further, commissioning the broader group of believers. In Mark 16:15–18, He said, *"Go into all the world and preach the gospel to every creature... And these signs will follow those who believe... they will lay hands on the sick, and they will recover."*

Scripture makes it clear that healing flows from Jesus' mission itself. *"For this purpose the Son of God was manifested, that He might destroy the works of the devil"* (1 John 3:8). After His resurrection, Jesus affirmed this continuity when He said, *"As the Father has sent Me, I also send you"* (John 20:21).

Healing, then, is not reserved for a select few—it is part of the Great Commission entrusted to all believers. Every member of the body of Christ is called to carry the compassion, authority, and power of Jesus into the world, bringing healing as a visible sign of the Kingdom of God.

Preparation for Ministry

Clear the Mechanism:

Before we come to church, we take inventory of both our own physical condition and emotional state. If we arrive with an existing issue—such as knee pain—and then sense knee pain while ministering, it can be difficult to discern whether that sensation is from the Holy Spirit or simply our own pain. In those moments, we ask the Holy Spirit to confirm the word in another way.

We also intentionally clear our emotional state by cultivating an atmosphere of honor through communion, worship, and praying in tongues. For us, this is a process of purity, because *"...the pure in heart shall see God"* (Matthew 5:8).

Forgiveness:

A key part of preparing for ministry is forgiving everyone and pursuing reconciliation where possible (Matthew 5:23–24; 6:14; Ephesians 4:32). We are called to forgive as the Lord has forgiven us, because we can only give what we ourselves possess. Scripture also reminds us that honor in our relationships matters deeply—1 Peter 3:7 instructs husbands to honor their wives so that nothing will hinder their prayers.

Create an Atmosphere of Honor:

Psalm 29:2 says, *"Honor the LORD for the glory of His name. Worship the LORD in the splendor of His holiness."* Honor requires intentional investment and pursuit of what God values most—even above our closest relationships. Honor leads us into true worship by anchoring our hearts' affection to Jesus and granting us access to what belongs to Him.

We honor Jesus through communion and remembering the price He paid for us. This posture produces repentance, brings cleansing to the soul, and often releases words of knowledge as a result of surrender and honor. Communion is not only for personal renewal; it is also a powerful tool for intercession on behalf of others (see Isaiah 53:5).

Through this process of purity, we are able to see what God is doing. And when we can see what God is doing, we recognize that He is inviting us to participate in His work.

Ministering to the Sick

John Sanford once said, *"Time is your friend, and haste is your enemy."* When we open the altar during a Sunday morning service, we are very aware of everything that still needs to happen once the time for prayer concludes. Even so, moving too quickly can lead us into error if we do not give the Holy Spirit time and room to do His work. There is no substitute for patience—take the time He requires.

We mentioned earlier that words of knowledge create faith. For this reason, we usually release words of knowledge immediately after worship, when hearts are surrendered to Jesus. If words of knowledge are shared at the end of a service, we intentionally re-enter worship to establish the same atmosphere for healing.

We have found that when words of knowledge are released, some are healed immediately, even without prayer, as they receive and respond in faith to the word spoken. Psalm 107:20 says, *"He sent out His word and healed them, rescuing them from the grave."* Words of knowledge ignite faith; they are the spark that starts the fire. Whether in a church service or a large crusade, releasing words of knowledge builds faith in the room. Instead of striving to stir yourself up, words of knowledge "prime the pump," allowing you to co-labor with the Holy Spirit by simply moving in what He is already doing.

After the words of knowledge are given, those receiving healing will come forward (or raise their hand), and the ministry leader will pray a brief prayer over the congregation. It is short because the word of knowledge has already released God's desire toward them—we are simply bearing witness to what He has initiated. Once faith has saturated the atmosphere, we typically invite the altar team to pray for those who received a word of knowledge. From there, we walk them through a few simple steps to receive their healing, similarly to what we have learned through Global Awakening.

Before people drift into the "flesh zone" and begin overanalyzing their condition, we encourage them to look for their healing by immediately moving what they could not move before. Then we ask anyone who is at least 70–80% better to wave their hand. We first saw Bill Johnson do this at Bethel Church, and it made perfect sense.

That simple act of waving builds faith, because it visibly demonstrates to the rest of the congregation that the Holy Spirit is honoring His word. When healing reaches the 70–80% mark, we remind everyone of Philippians 1:6 (NLT): *"And I am certain that God, who began the good work within you, will continue His work until it is finally finished."* God will finish what He starts. There is no need to wait for a full 100% in that moment—the Holy Spirit will complete what He starts. Typically, we see about 50% of the people healed after the first prayer.

Once the congregation witnesses the initial wave of healing, we press in again. In Mark 8:22–26, Jesus prayed twice for a blind man. After the first prayer, the man saw people "like trees walking." His healing was progressing but not yet complete, so Jesus prayed again—and the man was fully restored. In the second round, we ask the Holy Spirit for "more" and address any potential hindrances such as unforgiveness, spirits of infirmity, or affliction, commanding them to leave. Afterward, we again instruct people to test their healing and wave if they are now 70–80% better. Most often, the remaining 50% receive their healing at this point.

When we first began ministering this way, we saw about ten percent of the congregation healed. Over time, we have seen services where 25% of a congregation—we had a service where fifty people out of two hundred were healed in a single Sunday morning service.

Step One: The Interview

Be approachable and create an atmosphere where the person feels safe and at ease. Be sure to ask their name and what they would like prayer for. Ask about their physical condition, but avoid getting into excessive detail. As you gain experience, you will learn to identify issues more quickly, and your prayer approach will naturally adjust.

Explore a few key questions: Do they know the cause? Has it been diagnosed by a doctor, and if so, what was said? Does it run in their family? What was happening in their life when the condition began? Was there any trauma around that time? Is there anyone they may need to forgive?

As we ask these questions, we are listening carefully for the Holy Spirit to speak and give further insight. We also avoid touching the person at this stage, because stimulating the physical senses can keep them in the "flesh zone." Prayer is a spiritual action, and you want them attentive to what God is doing, not what they are physically feeling or perceiving.

These questions matter because sickness often has a root or a source. Where there is a symptom, there is a cause or where there is fruit, there is a root. For example, I struggled with allergies for most of my life. I love my dogs, yet I was allergic to them. Whenever I lay in bed at night and began to have an allergic reaction, I knew the dogs had been on my pillow during the day. One morning, as Kristen and I were getting ready for the day, she noticed me taking an allergy pill and asked when the allergies had first started. Surprisingly, I could not remember. As I thought about it, the memory suddenly surfaced—I was about four years old.

Kristen then asked if allergies ran in my family. I wasn't sure, so I called my mother. She confirmed that the allergies began when I was four and did not run in the family. Kristen further inquired about what had happened in my life at that age. Instantly, I remembered an incident I had completely forgotten for decades. When I was four, I was riding my bike home when a large black dog attacked me. The dog stood between me and my house, preventing me from going home. I had to use my bike as a shield to keep him from biting me. The ordeal lasted several minutes until a neighbor finally chased the dog away. About six months later, I was taken to the hospital, tested, and diagnosed with allergies to dogs.

What I realized was that my body remembered what my mind had tried to forget. Because the emotional wound was never resolved, encountering a dog triggered fear, which activated my hypothalamus to raise histamine levels, producing an allergic reaction designed to warn me to get away from dogs. (Dr. Henry Wright offers more insight on this connection in several of his books.)

Once the root was identified, my wife prayed a simple prayer with me. We forgave the dog—because forgiveness releases—bound the spirit of fear, commanded my hypothalamus to be reset, and spoke that my histamine levels would function as God intended. After that prayer, I went on with my day and didn't think much about it.

About a week later, I realized I had not experienced a single allergic reaction. I looked at my wife, and she smiled, thinking the same thing. She said, "I think you're healed." When I asked how she knew, she replied, "I let the dogs sleep on your pillow all week, and you never reacted once."

Step Two: Prayer Method

Choose the appropriate type of prayer you want to give in that moment—petition or command. Most people begin with a prayer of petition, which is a request directed to the Father, asking Jesus to heal. For example:

"Father, in the name of Jesus, I ask You to heal the pain in Ben's knee and remove all swelling and discomfort."

A prayer of command, however, is directed at the condition itself—whether a part of the body or a troubling spirit such as pain, infirmity, or affliction. When you are praying in response to a word of knowledge, a command is usually more appropriate, because a word of knowledge carries an authoritative release for healing or deliverance. For example: "In the name of Jesus, I command the pain in Ben's back to be healed and all swelling and pain to leave."

Step Three: Prayer Ministry

Begin by asking the Holy Spirit to come, and then wait on Him. We often feel rushed, but this is the moment to allow the Holy Spirit to do His work so you can do yours. Your role is to help the person focus on Jesus and to give the Holy Spirit room to move. Referred to as "getting them out of the flesh zone," natural thoughts, distractions, and self-awareness can interfere with healing. Help them adopt an attitude of receiving.

If the person approaching you is already praying to themselves, gently ask them to quiet their prayers and focus on Jesus, letting them know that you will be praying for them. Simple practical wisdom matters as well—be mindful of personal hygiene, as odorous distractions can make it difficult for someone to receive. They will have a hard time focusing if distracted by your bad breath. Avoid unnecessary physical contact, since prayer is a spiritual action and we do not want to cater to the flesh. If a catcher/usher, family member or spouse is touching them, I will have the person being prayed for lift their hands and ask the family member or spouse to quietly pray for them without touching them. In our church, an usher may stand behind the person and lightly tap their back so they know someone is there to support them if the power of the Holy Spirit causes them to drop.

Before you pray, discern whether forgiveness needs to take place. If the person—or the Holy Spirit—reveals unforgiveness, fear-based issues (such as allergies rooted in fear), autoimmune conditions connected to rejection or self-hatred, or generational patterns, forgiveness should come before praying for physical healing. At times, a physical condition is the outward symptom of an unresolved inner wound, trauma, or spiritual stronghold.

When you pray, keep your prayers short, specific, and in the name of Jesus. If you are a man praying for a woman, or a woman praying for a man, have them place their own hand on the area of pain, if needed, in order to maintain appropriate behavior. Keep your eyes open so you can observe how the Holy Spirit is moving and remain aware of what is happening around you. About half the people you pray for may feel heat, tingling, or a sensation like electricity. If this begins to happen, encourage them to tell you immediately.

Once you finish praying, instruct them not to analyze what they feel. Instead, have them move the area that was causing pain without hesitation. Encourage them to look for their healing, not for their pain.

If emotional or sensitive issues arise—especially those connected to sexual trauma or struggles—bring in someone of the same sex to continue ministering. A man should not minister alone to a woman in those situations, and a woman should not minister alone to a man. The safest and most effective environment is when men pray with men and women pray with women.

Step Four: Stop and Re-Interview

After they move the body part they could not move without pain before, pause, then reassess their condition. Ask whether there is improvement, no change, or if the pain has worsened or shifted.

Better:

Look for at least 80% improvement. This level of change confirms—both to me and to the person receiving prayer—that the Holy Spirit is actively manifesting healing. You do not need to see 100% immediately, because the Holy Spirit finishes what He begins (Philippians 1:6). If someone says, "I'm about 50% better," We will say out loud, "Holy Spirit, give them more," and pray again. After the second prayer, re-interview and reassess.

Worse:

If the pain worsens or moves to a different area of the body, this often indicates a spirit of affliction or torment. Immediately command the spirit to leave in the name of Jesus. After each command, reassess what is happening. For example, I once prayed for a woman with wrist pain. After prayer, the pain intensified and moved into her elbow. I commanded the spirit to leave, and it moved to her shoulder, then the other shoulder, then down the opposite arm and finally out of her body. I had to command it several times before it completely left.

Same:

If there is no change, return to the interview. Most often, unforgiveness is blocking the healing. Ask them to revisit when the condition began and to forgive everyone involved—including themselves. Some people carry guilt or shame and believe they deserve punishment, which can hinder healing. If there is still no change after prayer, seek the Holy Spirit for further insight. Some people are healed shortly after prayer, while others require deliverance because deeper issues are keeping them bound.

Additional Interview Questions:

Ask whether they can recall any significant event that occurred when the condition began. If this condition runs in the family, there may be a generational issue or curse that needs to be broken. Ask whether they or anyone in their family has participated in witchcraft, secret societies, or similar organizations. Has anyone ever spoken a curse over them or their family?

If nothing surfaces, ask about their birth. Was the pregnancy planned? Did the parents desire a different gender? Were there complications during childbirth? These questions can reveal unintentional words spoken over them or covenants that affected the child. For example, I once prayed for a young man who was hearing voices. I felt led to ask about his birth, and he said the umbilical cord was wrapped around his neck. I then asked if Freemasonry was present in his family. He said his grandfather was a Mason. In the first level of Freemasonry, a prophetic declaration is made with a cable-tow placed around the neck, and this young man was suffering the effects of that covenant and curse.

The re-interview stage is not about pressure or performance—it is about listening carefully to the Holy Spirit and discerning the root so true freedom and healing can take place.

Step Five: Post-Prayer Guidance

After prayer, encourage the person to remain consistent in their walk with the Lord. Reaffirm their identity in Christ and make sure they know they can reach out to you for support. If they received healing, remind them that the enemy may attempt to reintroduce symptoms to test their faith. If this happens, they should firmly command the pain to leave, declaring that they have been healed by the name and the blood of Jesus. We are not the sick trying to get well—we are the healthy, guarding our health.

If their healing is not yet complete, reassure them that healing is sometimes a process and that persistence matters (1 Timothy 1:18). This verse encourages us to take the word of knowledge and use it as a weapon of war. I have had people fight for a word after prayer and eventually receive their healing. Do not be discouraged if you don't see immediate results. Encourage them to continue coming forward for prayer and to stay connected to church, where God's grace and ongoing support are available to them.

Always minister from a place of love. The more people you pray for, the more you will learn, and the greater impact you will see in the lives of others.

Persistent Prayer: (see Luke 18:1–8)

Pray and do not lose heart. Consider the story of the demonized boy with seizures in Matthew 17:14–23. The disciples were unable to drive out the demon, and when they asked Jesus why, He replied, *"Because of the littleness of your faith."* The Greek word for "littleness" is *oligos*, meaning "short" or "brief." Jesus was not rebuking the size of their faith, but the duration of it. It was not about how much faith they had, but how long they were willing to stand in faith in the middle of the battle (see Matthew 13:5). Persistence is often the difference between a breakthrough delayed and a breakthrough received.

Progressive Healing:

John Wimber said, *"it's our job to lay hands on the sick, and Gods job is to heal."* We have seen many instances where people experienced no immediate relief at the altar, only to call hours or days later to say that Jesus had healed them. Healing does not always manifest instantly; at times, it unfolds progressively.

On one occasion, I received a word of knowledge for a woman experiencing pain in her foot, knee, and back. The word came as sensory pain. The pain in the foot was bad, then the pain in my knee was less and the pain in my hip and back was even less. Because of this, I understood that the issue in her foot was the root cause affecting her knee, hip and back. When she came forward, she explained that she had a floating bone in her foot that was pressing on a nerve. To compensate, she had altered the way she walked, which in turn caused strain in her knee, hip and back.

After I prayed for her, she experienced only slight relief and not a complete healing. I re-interviewed and led her through a prayer of forgiveness, and prayed again—yet there was still no noticeable change. Before she left, I told her that the Holy Spirit had clearly expressed His desire to heal her, and that she would need to hold onto the word she had received and continue to contend for it. 1 Timothy 1:18 (NLT) says, *"Timothy, my son, here are my instructions for you, based on the prophetic words spoken about you earlier. May they help you fight well in the Lord's battles."*

After that church service, each morning she continued her routine of walking her dog, but still in pain. Every day, she chose to thank Jesus for her healing. About a month later, she woke up completely pain-free. She went back to her doctor, and an MRI revealed that the floating bone in her foot was no longer there.

Common Hindrances to Healing

We began opening the altar for prayer as a regular routine immediately following worship. As we released words of knowledge, we witnessed the Holy Spirit move powerfully, and many people were healed. However, there were individuals who responded to the same words of knowledge week after week without any noticeable improvement. This led us to recognize the need to grow in our understanding of inner healing and deliverance.

I remember calling out what I believed to be ulcers in someone's stomach for two consecutive weeks. I was confident the Lord wanted to address it, yet no one responded. While teaching a class on words of knowledge, I mentioned this to the group. A woman seated in the front row slowly raised her hand, visibly ashamed, and said, "It's me." I reassured her and told her we would pray together at the end of the class.

After the class ended, I was speaking with a few students when I suddenly heard someone urgently call out, "Pastor Greg!" I turned and saw the woman standing completely rigid—she was stiff as a board and unable to move. As I looked at her, I had a vision of a white python coiled in her stomach. The word *python* in Greek (*pythōna*) is associated with divination (see Acts 16:16). As the snake lifted its head toward her right shoulder, I watched her shoulder twist inward, and I could see the pain etched on her face. The snake then moved toward her neck, and I saw her neck contort as her head tilted back toward the ceiling.

I had never witnessed anything like it. I genuinely feared her neck might snap at any moment. Her mouth was open in agony, tears streaming down her face, completely unable to resist what was happening. A righteous anger rose up inside me as I saw someone so helpless to fight. I immediately stepped forward, laid my hands on her neck, and in the name of Jesus, I commanded the demon to leave.

The power of God struck her, and she fell back into the front row of chairs. Even seated, her body remained rigid. I stood over her and looked into her eyes—and I could see eyes behind her eyes. I knew the demon had not yet left. I commanded it again to leave, and this time it did. Her body instantly relaxed, and I watched the peace of God settle over her as she began to sob—overwhelmed by freedom. Later, I learned that witchcraft had been present in her family line.

This experience reinforced an important truth: the Lord may reveal a physical condition, but there can also be emotional or spiritual strongholds attached to it which block healing. To keep things simple, I often ask the Holy Spirit one key question—whether the person is a captive or a prisoner?

Being Held a Captive or Prisoner

Isaiah 61:1 says, *"The Spirit of the Sovereign LORD is on me, because the LORD has anointed me to proclaim good news to the poor. He has sent me to bind up the brokenhearted, to proclaim **freedom for the captives** and **release from darkness for the prisoners...**"*

A **prisoner** is someone that is unwilling to forgive. Unforgiveness is one of the greatest obstacles to healing and deliverance. In the parable of the unforgiving servant (Matthew 18:21–35), a servant who had been forgiven of an enormous debt refused to forgive a much smaller one. Because he would not forgive, the king handed him over to the "tormentors" until the debt was paid in full (Matthew 18:34). These tormentors represent demonic oppression. Forgiveness does not mean you must trust the person who wounded you; it means you trust God to be your judge and restorer. Forgiveness is not for the offender's benefit—it is for your freedom. It is an act of faith that severs the tie to both the offense and the offender. Forgiveness is also strategic. If you want to grow to your next level, your future demands it.

Through unforgiveness, spirits of infirmity (sickness) can gain access to a person's life, along with bitterness, anger, rebellion, witchcraft, generational curses, soul ties, wounds from the womb, and other forms of spiritual bondage. Proverbs 26:2 (NLT) says, *"Like a fluttering sparrow or a darting swallow, an undeserved curse will not land on its intended victim."* Unforgiveness creates a place for curses to land, settle, and remain.

In many ministry sessions, we have had to tell individuals that if they are seeking true freedom, then forgiveness is not optional—it is essential. Unforgiveness grants demonic forces legal access to torment a person. When someone refuses to forgive, they are effectively giving the tormentors permission to remain (Matthew 18:34). When a person chooses not to forgive, we bless them and release them, knowing that freedom cannot come until forgiveness is embraced.

A **captive** is also placed behind bars when they believe a lie and empower the liar. Their struggle is not primarily with unforgiveness, but with false beliefs about themselves, their condition, their past or about God.

For the captive, the truth of God's promises must be affirmed and revealed. John 8:32 says, *"You will know the truth, and the truth will set you free."* The word *know* speaks of experiential knowledge—revelation that comes only through the Holy Spirit. In this passage, *truth* means reality. A person's sense of reality is shaped by the environment and atmosphere they continually expose themselves to, and that reality becomes the lens through which they see everything through. Truth, then, is not only God's perspective; it is the ultimate and superior reality. Faith is simply learning to see everything—especially ourselves—through God's eyes. It is this revelation of truth that frees the captive from bondage and brings them into liberty in Christ. This is what it means to have the mind of Christ. As Scripture says, *"As a man thinks in his heart, so is he"* (Proverbs 23:7).

Captives often live under guilt, shame, condemnation, fear, anxiety, oppression, depression, inner vows, rejection, poverty, self-hatred, curses, and/or self-imposed curses. Unresolved fear can open the door to conditions such as allergies and asthma, as you witnessed occurred during my contact with dogs. Self-hatred or bitterness can become a self-fulfilling prophecy and may open the door to autoimmune disorders such as rheumatoid arthritis, multiple sclerosis, and Crohn's disease.

Several years ago, I had a dream of a man entering a house that was in severe disrepair. The paint was peeling, and the exterior looked as though it were melting. The man opened the front door and instructed his son to go in first, then followed him inside. About a month later, a family contacted me to help sell their home. When my wife and I met them to present an offer, the husband said, "We didn't just hire you to sell our house." When I asked what else they needed, he explained that his wife had suffered from arthritis in her spine for sixteen years and that he knew I prayed for the sick.

His wife, a believer, confirmed that she had been prayed for many times at church, with no relief. I told her I would not pray for her at that moment. Many people want healing without revelation—they want the pain removed without addressing the root cause. Sometimes a wound must be reopened before it can be properly cleaned and healed. So, in that moment I needed to explain the deeper cause of her chronic pain.

I have often observed that back problems are connected to unresolved anger and bitterness towards others. Unknown to them, God had already given me insight through the dream about the husband, and the Holy Spirit quickly brought the pieces together. What they thought was their idea—inviting us over for prayer, the Holy Spirit had already pre-arranged. Remember, as a seer, God often provides information in advance. Although, we may not be able to make sense of it at first.

I asked the husband if I could speak candidly, and he agreed. I told him that he had been involved in gambling and pornography, which had caused significant financial strain on the family. As a result, his wife had grown bitter toward him. In the dream, when the father opened the door for the firstborn son, the Lord was revealing that this was a generational issue. Scripture teaches that certain sins can affect multiple generations (Exodus 20:5; Deuteronomy 23:2). I explained that this pattern had already begun to affect their son, but that Jesus could set their family free.

Kristen and I first addressed the husband's issue. We had him renounce pornography and gambling and took him through a short prayer for restoration. We then broke the generational curse off the son. After they were free, we began ministering to his wife as unforgiveness led to bitterness and bitterness to the infirmity in her back. After several minutes, the wife was willing to forgive her husband and we had her sit on the couch between me and my wife. I told her, "Watch how easy this is." I said this because the legal tie and attachment to her infirmity had been broken through forgiveness. I took one finger, placed it on her forehead and said, "Jesus, heal her." She said fire immediately went down her spine and for the first time in 16 years, she was free of pain.

A Word of Encouragement

Kristen and I were in Brazil with my eldest son, ministering words of knowledge and praying for the sick with the Global Awakening team. At the time, my son Eli was only eighteen years old, so he accompanied me with an interpreter as I ministered to the sick most of the time. I use the prayer model as a guide and oftentimes I go right after the issue by asking about the root cause. In one instance, a boy came to me covered in hives. As soon as I heard about his hives, I knew to start with light deliverance as his issue was rooted in fear. Once deliverance is complete, we typically will pray for healing.

Through the interpreter, I told the boy's father that this was not simply a healing issue, but a deliverance issue, because fear was triggering elevated histamine levels. After guiding both father and son to renounce fear, I prayed for healing, and the boy immediately began to experience relief.

Eli continued to accompany me as we moved through the crowd, watching me pray differently for each person as the Holy Spirit led me. I knew after he saw me minister healing and deliverance to a few people, he was a bit overwhelmed. I encouraged him to keep pressing in, reminding him that God would use him at his current level of revelation and would continue to grow him into what He had called him to be.

One night, we were at the front of the altar and giving out words of knowledge to a Brazilian congregation of about three thousand members. Eli received a word of knowledge about back problems, and after his spoke it over the church, five people came forward for prayer. He looked at me and said, "Dad, what do I do? I can't do what you do." I told him, "Do what you know to do. If Jesus revealed it, He plans to heal it. Use the name of Jesus, operate at your level of revelation, and command the sick to be healed. The Holy Spirit will use you right where you are at." Later, Eli came back and told me that four out of the five people had left the altar with at least eighty percent relief in their back.

We all have to start somewhere in healing and deliverance. We must move in the revelation we have, trusting that the Holy Spirit will meet us there. We cannot wait until we feel fully equipped or knowledgeable before ministering to the sick and afflicted. I explained to Eli that as his gift grows, God will expand his capacity and place greater demand on him. That is why I emphasize this principle: minister at your level of revelation, and the Holy Spirit will show up.

Chapter 7 – Set Them Free

John 8:32 says, *"You will know the truth, and the truth will make you free."* To *know* is to perceive or experience, and *truth* is reality. Reality is the world as it actually exists, and each of us forms our sense of reality through experience—both good and bad. From those experiences, we seek order, and through order we pursue our own "truth."

In 2009, I arrived at church early for pre-service prayer. The atmosphere was unusually quiet, so I began asking people how they were doing. Senior Pastor Derron pulled me aside and told me that one of the youth—let's call him Justin—had manifested a demon at a youth event the night before. Internally, I struggled to believe this. Justin was saved and had been involved with the youth group for a couple of years.

Pastor Derron explained that during worship the previous evening, Justin suddenly stood up and began calling out the sins of others. The youth leaders quickly recognized this as demonic and restrained him while praying for several hours, believing the demon had left. Pastor Derron then said to me, "If Justin comes in this morning and he isn't free, I need you to take care of him." At that time, I had very little formal understanding of deliverance, though I had been praying for the sick and had experienced both demonic and angelic encounters since I was about four years old.

As worship began, Justin walked into the church and went straight to the altar. He appeared to be in a trance, completely fixated on the worship team. I stepped in front of him and said, "Justin, sit down on the front row." Without breaking his gaze or showing any expression, he obeyed. The moment he sat down, his body became rigid, his eyes rolled back, and he began to shake.

I stood in front of him and said, "Justin, stand up and go to the foyer." Demons thrive on attention, disruption, and public embarrassment, so it was important to remove him from the service while keeping the congregation focused on Jesus. Again, without expression, Justin stood up and walked toward the foyer. As we walked, I asked the Holy Spirit what to do, and I heard clearly, *"Tell him to forgive her."*

When we reached the foyer, I stood in front of Justin and could see yellow eyes behind his eyes. I addressed the demon and said, "So, you like messing with little kids, huh?" There was no response. Then I said, "Justin, forgive her." He shouted, "I forgive her!" As he said it, his body began to shake violently then he collapsed. As he collapsed, I caught him by the front of his shirt and guided him down into a chair. Justin immediately began to cry and was completely free.

Later, I learned that Justin had been falsely accused of rape by a girl and expelled from school. The unresolved anger and unforgiveness opened the door to bitterness, which in turn gave the enemy access and a foothold in his life.

That experience forced me to confront a theological tension. What I witnessed did not align with what I had been taught about demons. I had to decide whether my experience was wrong or my doctrine was incomplete. I could not deny what I had seen, so I had to reexamine my theology. Many who have been taught that a believer cannot have both the Holy Spirit and a demon must wrestle with real-life experiences that do not support that conclusion.

Scripture says, *"May the God of peace make you holy in every way, and may your whole spirit and soul and body be kept blameless until our Lord Jesus Christ comes again"* (1 Thessalonians 5:23). Many believe that once a person is saved, the enemy can no longer take up any residence in their life. I would invite those individuals to observe almost any altar call. People come forward for sickness, anxiety, depression, brokenness, hopelessness—conditions that often require deliverance as much as healing. When the church dismisses the reality of evil, it becomes ill-equipped to confront it.

You *are* a spirit, you *have* a soul, and you *live* in a body. At salvation, the Holy Spirit takes residence in your spirit, and Satan is expelled. However, the enemy can still exert influence in the soul—through fear, anxiety, and oppression—and in the body through affliction or infirmity. Some argue that the Holy Spirit and the devil cannot occupy the same space, yet in Job 2:1 we see Satan presenting himself before God among the angels. Regardless, it is God's desire is to occupy and bring wholeness to your entire being—spirit, soul, and body.

Deliver Us From Evil

Jesus instructed us to pray in Matthew 6:13, *"But deliver us from evil."* The word *evil* represents the full curse of sin upon humanity. The Greek word *ponēros* (evil) is derived from *ponos*, meaning hardship or pain, which in turn comes from *penēs*, meaning poor. The progression is clear: sin leads to pain, and pain often results in poverty or lack. In this single word, Scripture captures the destructive cycle of evil—sin, sickness, and poverty.

Deliverance is defined as "the act of being rescued or set free from bondage or danger." The root meaning of *deliver* is to liberate—to set free, even to assist in giving birth. Biblically, deliverance involves the casting out of unclean spirits and the restoration of wholeness. It is an essential part of "working out your own salvation," as described in Philippians 2:12. The word translated *salvation* in that verse is *sōtēria*, which Thayer's Lexicon defines as "deliverance from the molestation of enemies." Salvation, therefore, is not merely a moment but a process of ongoing freedom.

Approximately one-third of Jesus' earthly ministry was devoted to deliverance. Acts 10:38 states, *"God anointed Jesus of Nazareth with the Holy Spirit and with power. Then Jesus went around doing good and healing all who were oppressed by the devil, for God was with Him."* The word *oppressed* conveys the idea of being pressed down, crushed, or burdened—often affecting the heart, emotions, and inner life.

In both biblical and practical terms, deliverance is the ministry of setting people free from bondage, danger, and spiritual oppression. It is the expression of God's power to restore what has been bound, broken, or stolen. This is the biblical foundation for deliverance.

1. **The Children's Bread: Mark 7:24-30**. Jesus said, *"It is not good to take the children's bread and throw it to the dogs."* Deliverance is for God's covenant believers. The *bread* represents healing, deliverance, salvation. The *dogs* represent non-believers (Gentiles). Jesus can get you free but you may not have the power and authority to stay free. The grace and mercy you receive to get free is the same grace and mercy you will need to walk in to maintain your freedom. This is why we feel it is crucial to maintain a relationship with God and church during the pathway to salvation.

2. **Luke 13:10-13,16** *"On a Sabbath, Jesus was teaching in one of the synagogues, and a woman was there who had been crippled by a spirit for eighteen years. She was bent over and could not straighten up at all. When Jesus saw her, he called her forward and said to her, 'Woman, you are set free from your infirmity.' Then he put his hands on her, and immediately she straightened up and praised God...The woman was a **daughter of Abraham**."* Infirmity is usually the manifestation of inequity (sin) from a generational curse and appears as an affliction in the flesh. Deliverance is a part of the salvation package that appropriates the work of Jesus on Calvary using the:

1. **Word of God:** (Matthew 8:8, 24:35, Hebrews 4:12, 2 Corinthians 4:3-4)
2. **Name of Jesus:** (Luke 10:17, Acts 16:16-18)
3. **Blood of Jesus:** (Exodus 12:13, Revelation 12:11)

The use of the Word, the Name of Jesus, and the Blood of Jesus breaks curses, strongholds, and bondages, and includes the casting out of evil spirits, commonly called demons. This is accomplished through prayer and fasting, and by exercising the authority to bind and loose, as taught by Jesus in Matthew 17:21 and Matthew 18:18 (AMP).

Physical Illness and Demons

Not all sickness or disease is caused by demons. Scripture clearly distinguishes between those who are physically or mentally ill and those who are demonized. In the New Testament, demons are mentioned approximately eighty times, and in at least eleven of those references, a clear distinction is made between illnesses caused by demonic influence and those arising from other factors. By walking someone through the process of healing, we can discern the symptom in order to identify the underlying cause and minister appropriately toward their restoration.

1 Thessalonians 5:23 says, *"May God himself, the God of peace, sanctify you completely. May your whole spirit, soul, and body be kept blameless at the coming of our Lord Jesus Christ."*

1. **Mind:** Capacity to think.
2. **Will:** Capacity to choose.
3. **Emotion:** Capacity to feel.

3 John 1:2 states, *"Beloved, I pray that you may prosper in all things and be in health, just as your soul prospers."* Health in Greek is *hugiaino*, meaning "all parts working together without debilitating sickness."

1. Health is functioning *holistically* with all parts *working together*. Meaning, there is a connection with spirit, soul and body. Health is determined by the unity we have in our body, soul and spirit.
2. Psalm 31:9 ESV states, *"Be gracious to me, O LORD, for I am in distress; my eye is wasted from grief; my soul and my body also."* What you see and constantly expose yourself to is the reality you choose to create. The reality you create impacts your emotions and your physical health.
3. Proverbs 4:23 says, *"Above all else, guard your heart for everything you do comes from it."*
4. Proverbs 23:7 also states, *"As a man thinks in his heart, so is he."*

In Luke 13:11 there was a woman who was crippled by an evil spirit or what the bible calls a "spirit of infirmity" for eighteen years. She walked bent over and could not straighten up at all. Jesus laid his hands on her and set her free from her infirmity. Infirmity is a physical sickness with a demonic source caused by sin. Being healed of an infirmity is understood as the removal of a demonic or spiritual hindrance in the flesh that originated from sin. When a man was brought to Jesus who was blind in John 9, the disciples asked, *"Rabbi, who sinned, this man or his parents that he was born blind?"*

The common belief was that sickness came upon man when he sinned *(Romans 5:12).*

Psalm 38:3,5 says, *"There is no soundness in my flesh because of your anger; there is no health in my bones because of my sin."*

After Jesus healed the cripple at the pool of Bethesda, Jesus told him in John 5:14, *"See you are well again. Stop sinning or something worse may happen to you."*

Through Jesus, there is forgiveness of sin. Psalm 103:3 says, *"He forgives all your inequities (sin) and heals all your diseases."*

Romans 10: 13 says, *"Whoever calls upon the name of the Lord will be saved."* Salvation is *sozo* in the Greek. Salvation delivers you, forgives you and heals you emotionally and physically.

Your body was designed with the ability to heal itself. In the medical field, a person is typically considered sick when there is a malfunction in the body. Take a broken bone, for example—a doctor does not actually heal the bone. Instead, the doctor sets it back into proper alignment, trusting that the body will do what it was created to do—repair *itself*. In the same remarkable way, the soul is "reset" through repentance, bringing it back into alignment so healing and restoration can take place.

Emotional and Mental Health

Psalm 139:14 declares, *"I praise You, for I am fearfully and wonderfully made; marvelous are Your works, and my soul knows it very well."*

Many struggles with sickness and disease have spiritual and emotional roots tied to broken relationships—with God, others, and within ourselves. A significant number of people wrestle with self-hatred, self-rejection, and the belief that they are unlovable. When emotional wounds remain unhealed—whether caused by personal sin, being sinned against, or generational patterns—they produce lasting consequences in a person's life, emotionally and physically.

One common perspective assumes that mental and emotional conditions exist solely because of chemical imbalances in the brain. While medication may reduce symptoms, if the imbalance was triggered by trauma, loss, or emotional injury, medication alone cannot cure the underlying cause. As a result, true healing is often incomplete. Inner healing has physical outworkings. Just as a bone must be properly set to heal, when a person receives the right emotional "reset" through the redemptive power of the cross, the soul can begin to realign, and restoration in spirit, soul, and body can follow.

Although salvation itself is a profound act of healing, not every aspect of a person's healing is completed at conversion. This is why Philippians 2:12 exhorts us to "work out" our salvation with fear and trembling. The word "salvation" in the Greek is *soteria* in this passage which includes both salvation and deliverance—freedom from the oppression and interference of the enemy.

When addressing the spirit and the soul, we are often speaking of what is commonly called inner healing. Many who seek physical healing are not only afflicted in their bodies but also wounded in their souls. Jesus acknowledged that people can be made sick through spiritual oppression, often described in Scripture as unclean or evil spirits.

There is a strong connection between the soul and the body, between healing prayer and dealing honestly with sin and belief systems. Feelings are important, but they are meant to be servants, not masters. Genesis 4:7 warns, *"If you do well, will you not be accepted? And if you do not do well, sin is crouching at the door; its desire is for you, but you must rule over it."* Deuteronomy 28:60 says, *"He will bring on you all the diseases of Egypt that you dreaded, and they will cling to you."* You are the healthy called to protect your health. God's perfect will is not to heal you. His perfect will is that you obey his voice and do not get sick.

On many occasions, we have prayed for healing after receiving words of knowledge, yet the sick did not recover. It was in our pursuit of Jesus that we were instructed to go further into deliverance and inner healing to find the root cause of the sickness and see those that are afflicted get well.

We have received a words of knowledge for healing and we later realized we were dealing with a spirit of infirmity. As I told in one story, I received a word of knowledge for a woman about a stomach issue or what I believed were ulcers and she manifested a demon because of generational witchcraft. In another meeting, I had a similar word of knowledge for a stomach issue and the Lord spoke to me about the man and said, "He is a witch and hates himself enough to kill himself." He showed up to my church, received Jesus and was delivered from the demon(s) that afflicted him and was ultimately healed of his stomach issue.

We have prayed for healing for several people with asthma and allergies with no results. When we understood to follow the fruit to the root and ask a few more questions, we understood that fear was the underlying cause of both conditions and we would initiate with a prayer for deliverance by dealing with the cause and not the symptom. Once a person was delivered we would circle back around and pray for healing and see the sick become well.

Autoimmune disorders start off as a break-down in relationships whereas rejection lies at the root. Rejection is a denial of love. When a person believes they are unloved, self-hatred begins to set in and it becomes a demonic stronghold. Because of rejection and self-hatred, when a person suffers with things like Rheumatoid Arthritis, Multiple Sclerosis and Crohn's Disease, their emotional disorder has caused their own body to attack themselves. When the issue remains unresolved, the autoimmune disorder can become a genetic disorder or what the bible calls a generational curse (Exodus 20:5-6, Numbers 14:18).

Your healing can be found through forgiveness of God, people and self. Personalizing, confessing, and believing Psalm 139 will bring a right "reset" to your emotions and heal your body. Psalm 139:16 says, "*You saw me before I was born. Every day of my life was recorded in your book. Every moment was laid out before a single day had passed."*

When you believe and act on what Jesus says about you, truth is forged into your heart and transformation in your mind accelerates. When you believe and act on lies spoken over you—by others or by yourself—you become captive to those lies, laying a foundation for bondage and strongholds.

What are Demons?

The story of demons begins as far back as Genesis. Demons are disembodied evil spirits desiring to have bodies through which to manifest their own evil lustful motives. Here are a few factors to take into consideration when understanding demons:

- Demons are disembodied spirits who rebelled against the Lord during the insurrection of Lucifer (Rev 12:3-4, 7-10, Isaiah 14:3-5, 12-17, Ezekiel 28:13-19, Luke 10:18, 2 Peter 2:4, Jude 1:6)
- Jude 1:6 says, "*And the angels who did not keep their positions of authority but abandoned their proper dwelling—these he has kept in darkness, bound with everlasting chains for judgment on the great day."*
- Demons operate under the direction and control of Satan. The goal of these spirits is to harass, torment, frustrate, and cause hardship for man.
- Demons can only operate under the dominion and power you give them. Sin creates a door for them to enter a person's life regardless if you are saved or not. Once inside the heart/mind of a person, they tempt, deceive, accuse, condemn, pressure, defile, resist, oppose, control, steal, affect, kill and destroy.

The New Testament Greek word for "demon" is *daimonion,* often translated as "devil" or described as being "demonized," meaning under the influence or power of demons. Christians cannot be *demon-possessed,* because possession implies ownership. Scripture is clear that ownership belongs to God alone: "*Behold, all souls are Mine"* (Ezekiel 18:4). For this reason, the more accurate term is *demonized.* A helpful analogy is this: I may give you the keys to *drive* my car, but that does not mean you *own* my car. You are simply operating something you have been given access to.

A believer can be demonized when an area of the heart has not been submitted to the cross of Jesus. When parts of our lives remain unyielded, trust in God is compromised, creating division or "emotional cracks" in the heart. Scripture warns that every crack can become a foothold for the enemy (Ephesians 4:27). This foothold is an unresolved area of agreement with sin, trauma where lies take root, unforgiveness or fleshly things that allow the enemy influence—but not yet dominion. If left without repentance, a foothold can develop into a stronghold—a place where the enemy is allowed to remain. The stronghold then becomes a fortified mindset or pattern. Another way of looking at it is this way: A foothold is like a door left unlocked or open. A stronghold is where the enemy is now moving decrepit furniture in and claiming space.

Many believers experience a plateau in their walk with Christ because these unaddressed areas limit spiritual growth. There is often a longing for "more," yet progress stalls out. In His love, God may withhold promotion or blessing, not as punishment, but to protect us. He does not want our nets to break or our boat to sink under the weight of responsibility (see Luke 5:6). If promotion comes while cracks still exist, the added weight of responsibility will make the cracks grow bigger. God prefers to deal with issues in private before they are exposed in public.

By carefully walking someone through the process of healing, we can discern symptoms, identify root causes, and cooperate with God's restorative work in their life. If it is in fact an emotional crack evolving into a stronghold, then this is where inner healing and deliverance is required.

Fallen Angels

Fallen angels rebelled, alongside Satan, against God. Although they retain their angelic nature, they have been stripped of their original power and authority (Isaiah 14:12–15; Revelation 12:3–4, 7–9; Ezekiel 28:12–17). Angels occupy positions of cosmic or territorial authority—often described as principalities operating in the "second heaven"—while demons function at a personal, ground-level capacity, interacting with and attempting to influence human lives. Angels carry strategies that affect regions, whereas demons focus on strategies of affliction and bondage directed at individuals.

In the ministry of deliverance, we deal with demons, not fallen angels. Even so, both have already been defeated. Colossians 2:15 declares, *"And having disarmed the powers and authorities, He made a public spectacle of them, triumphing over them by the cross."* All spiritual powers are subject to Christ's authority.

This authority is also delegated to believers. In Luke 10:17–20, the seventy returned with joy, saying, *"Lord, even the demons are subject to us in Your name."* Jesus replied, *"I saw Satan fall like lightning from heaven. Behold, I give you authority to trample on serpents and scorpions, and over all the power of the enemy, and nothing shall by any means hurt you. Nevertheless, do not rejoice in this, that the spirits are subject to you, but rather rejoice because your names are written in heaven."*

Believers are therefore called to stand in confidence, not fear (Ephesians 6:10–18; 2 Timothy 1:7). Scripture reminds us in 1 John 3:8, *"For this purpose the Son of God was manifested, that He might destroy the works of the devil."* If this was Jesus' mission, it is also ours. As Jesus affirmed, *"Peace to you! As the Father has sent Me, I also send you"* (John 20:21).

Strongholds

"Or again, how can anyone enter a strong man's house and carry off his possessions unless he first ties up the strong man? Then he can plunder his house" (Matthew 12:29).

For though we walk in the flesh, we are not waging war according to the flesh. For the weapons of our warfare are not of the flesh (carnal/self-made defense mechanisms) but have divine power to destroy strongholds. We destroy arguments and every lofty opinion raised against the knowledge of God, and take every thought captive to obey Christ, being ready to punish every disobedience, when your obedience is complete (2 Corinthians 10:3-6).

The repetitious response to pain or pressure is called a stronghold. A **stronghold** can be understood as a fortress—an area of life dominated or occupied by a particular influence. In the Greek, the idea carries the meaning *"to make firm,"* referring to misplaced confidence in human strength rather than trust in God. Strongholds are built as a way to create a sense of safety, control, or ease of movement, but they are ultimately carnal coping mechanisms that violate reliance on the Lord. A stronghold forms when a person attempts to protect themselves in their own strength. Over time, willpower proves insufficient, and the very thing a person tries to protect themselves from becomes the thing they continue to receive from.

*"Our God is in the heavens; he does all that he pleases. Their idols are silver and gold, the work of human hands. They have mouths, but do not speak; eyes, but do not see. They have ears, but do not hear; noses, but do not smell. They have hands, but do not feel; feet, but do not walk; and they do not make a sound in their throat. Those who make them **become like them; so do all who trust in them**."* (Psalm 115:3-8)

What you continually think about is what you value. What you value is what you honor, and what you honor is what you invest in. What you invest in becomes what you worship. When worship is directed toward anything other than God, it becomes misplaced worship.

In Judges 6:10 (NLT), the Lord says, *"I told you, 'I am the LORD your God. You must not worship the gods of the Amorites, in whose land you now live.' But you have not listened to me."* The NKJV reads, *"Do not fear the gods of the Amorites… But you have not obeyed My voice."* The Hebrew word for "fear" here is *yare*, meaning reverence or deep respect—honor that leads to obedience and worship. This reveals why fear and worship are closely connected: what you continually fear is what you worship. Honor and worship give access—both ways. What you worship gives you access to what it possesses, but it also gains access to you. When fear opens the door to demonic influence, you no longer control what enters or how it operates in your life. Yet all of this can be repented of, and strongholds can be removed in the mighty name of Jesus.

For example, a person who experienced rejection at birth may develop isolation as a coping mechanism because it feels safe. While isolation may protect them from potential harm, it also keeps out the very people God may use to bring healing, protection, and freedom. Demonic strongholds violate trust in God by keeping Him out of areas of the heart while granting the enemy freedom of movement in a person's life.

A stronghold can also be defined as an ingrained, repetitive thought pattern—one your mind habitually follows. It shapes how you think, how you respond, and how you behave. Repeatedly traveling down these thought pathways is like driving a truck down a dirt road. Over time, deep ruts form, and eventually, little effort is needed to stay in those ruts—you simply align the tires and accelerate (as described by Rodney Hogue in his book, *Liberated*).

Trauma often occurs when a situation is interpreted solely through natural eyes rather than spiritual ones. Healing from trauma, and freedom from strongholds come when we learn to see events through God's perspective. Trauma can plant the lie that Jesus was absent, producing hopelessness. Trauma itself does not always open the door to demonic influence, but the repeated coping responses used to avoid pain often do. What begins as a fleshly response can eventually become a demonic stronghold.

Matthew 13:30, in the parable of the wheat and the tares, offers an important principle. While the men slept, the enemy sowed tares among the wheat. Jesus' instruction was to allow both to grow together until the harvest. This speaks to maturity. God delivered Israel from Egypt in one day, yet it took forty years to remove Egypt from Israel's heart. Likewise, many people cannot release a stronghold until they mature in the freedom made available through the cross. When given a choice between a *known bondage* and an *unknown freedom*, most will choose the familiar bondage. It is through deliverance and discipleship that believers mature enough in Christ to allow the separation of wheat from chaff and walk fully in freedom.

Inner Healing

Matthew 12:43–45 and Luke 11:24–26 say: *"When an unclean spirit goes out of a man, it passes through dry places seeking rest and finds none. Then it says, 'I will return to my house from which I came.' When it returns, it finds the house empty, swept, and put in order. Then it goes and brings with it seven other spirits more wicked than itself, and they enter and live there. And the final condition of that person is worse than the first."*

Deliverance by itself is not enough. When dealing with demonic influence, it is essential to identify what allowed the "house" to be built into a demonic stronghold in the first place. If the root issues are not addressed—such as unforgiveness, trauma, or unhealthy character patterns—the enemy will eventually find a way back in. When these roots are forgiven, exposed, and put to death at the cross, the demon's dwelling place is dismantled, leaving nothing for it to return to.

Inner healing is therefore a vital component of deliverance. A helpful analogy is this: if someone is stabbed in the arm, deliverance removes the knife (demon), but inner healing cleans and treats the wound (stronghold). Inner healing reveals and closes the wounds that originally opened the door for the enemy's access. While a demon can be cast out through deliverance, failure to resolve the underlying wound, open door, or stronghold, allows it to return—often with greater force, just as Jesus warned in Matthew 12:43–45. We will go deeper into the process of inner healing later in this chapter.

Evangelizing Unbelieving Hearts

Philippians 2:12 instructs us to *"continue to work out your salvation with fear and trembling."* The word "salvation" here is *soteria*, which includes deliverance from the molestation and influence of the enemy. *Soteria* also means preservation and wholeness, so simply put, continue to work towards achieving wholeness.

Hebrews 12:15 warns us to *"see to it that no one falls short of the grace of God and that no root of bitterness springs up and causes trouble, and by it many become defiled."* Bitterness always begins with unforgiveness. Unforgiveness allows that root to take place in in the soil of the heart, planting a seed of bitterness.

When we first received Jesus as Lord and Savior, His finished work on the cross became our finished work as well (John 19:30). From that moment forward, we were called to enforce His victory, not to fight for it. At the cross, our sins were forgiven and our flesh was crucified—but the challenge is that the flesh refuses to stay dead. This is what Scripture refers to as a root "springing up." What was put to death at salvation can attempt to revive if it is not continually submitted to the cross, bringing defilement to both ourselves and others.

Inner healing is the intentional, Spirit-led process of going beneath the surface to identify any roots that are trying to come back to life and bringing them fully and finally to the cross. Through this process, those roots are rendered powerless, allowing Christ's victory to be fully expressed in our lives. Proverbs 25:3 declares, *"As the heavens are high and the earth is deep, so the hearts of kings are unsearchable."*

One reason we do not always live out what Jesus instructs is that deep within our hearts there can still be areas of unbelief. Inner healing is an act of obedience to the cautionary verse in Hebrews: *"Take care, brethren, that there not be in any one of you an evil, unbelieving heart that falls away from the living God"* (Hebrews 3:12).

As a Christian man, when I personally went through deliverance, the Holy Spirit brought to the surface five traumatic experiences—known as *suppressed memories*. After each incident occurred, it was pushed out of awareness and buried. One of these memories took place when I was about eight years old and sent to stay with my grandmother for a few weeks during the summer. One day she took me and my brother to her friend's house where people were drinking and playing cards. She locked us in a small room so that she could play cards most of the day. Hours passed, we were hungry, and we had been told not to leave the room.

Eventually, my grandmother returned, but she was clearly drunk and could barely walk. She struggled to unlock the car door, and for reasons I still don't fully understand, I helped her get the key into the lock so we could leave. She insisted she was fine to drive, yet she struggled to get the key into the ignition. My brother and I sat in the back seat, terrified. As I later revisited this memory, I recognized thoughts I had unknowingly carried since that day: *Why would my parents allow this? Will we make it home alive? Why is no one fighting for us?*

Trauma

Trauma often remains because we walk away from the experience of believing a lie. When the Holy Spirit led me back to this moment, during deliverance, I suddenly saw Jesus sitting in the back seat between me and my brother. As I observed the scene, I realized that the only reason we made it home safely was because He was there. He had His arm around me and gently said, "You are going to be okay." I watched as He reached forward, took hold of the steering wheel, and corrected the car's direction several times until we arrived home safely.

This revelation was profoundly significant. It established a deep love-relationship with Jesus by showing me that in my worst moments I was never alone, never forgotten, and always worth fighting for.

After the Holy Spirit walked me through all five suppressed traumatic experiences, I saw what appeared to be five rings floating in front of me, as though it were on a T.V. screen. Then I saw something like a silver needle or rocket with a long thread trailing behind it. Inscribed on its side was the word *insignificance*. It pierced through all five rings, tying them together. The Holy Spirit revealed that the same wound connected all of those events, and at the root of insignificance was rejection. In that moment, rejection broke off my life. I felt as though a tremendous weight had lifted, and I walked away genuinely free, knowing deep in my heart that I am a son and that God accepts me just as I am. From that point forward, I no longer struggled with my identity, and the power of God began to flow more freely in my ministry. We must learn to live in right relationship with God as sons and daughters—not with a servant mindset or an orphan mentality.

Why don't all believers walk in freedom? Because hidden areas of the heart can prevent the fullness of the Good News from reaching every part of our lives. While we may have responded to an altar call and had our spirit made right with God, not all of our soul and flesh are instantly transformed. Some areas remain untouched—either through ignorance of God's grace or an inward resistance to it. Inner healing is a vital part of deliverance ministry, bringing the Gospel to those parts of a believer's heart that have not yet fully believed or surrendered to Christ.

Inner healing is, in essence, evangelizing the unbelieving hearts of believers. It is the application of the death and resurrection life of our Lord Jesus Christ to those stubborn dimensions of the heart that have so far resisted the redemption our minds and spirits welcomed when we first invited Jesus in.

Romans 10:9–10 says, *"If you confess with your mouth, 'Jesus is Lord,' and believe in your heart that God raised Him from the dead, you will be saved. For with the heart one believes and is justified, and with the mouth one confesses and is saved."* The Gospel cannot be fully lived if it is believed only in the mind. It must be experienced in the heart, for it is the truth we *know*—by experience—that sets us free (John 8:32).

The Process of Crucifixion

"I have been crucified with Christ and I no longer live, but Christ lives in me. The life I now live in the body, I live by faith in the Son of God, who loved me and gave Himself for me" (Galatians 2:20).

Inner healing is the ongoing process of taking up our cross daily and allowing the Lord to put to death the remaining areas of our fallen nature as He reveals them. Before Jesus washed the disciples' feet in John 13:7–10, He said, *"You do not realize now what I am doing, but later you will understand."* Peter immediately objected, saying, *"You shall never wash my feet."* Jesus replied, *"Unless I wash you, you have no part with Me."* Peter then asked Jesus to wash his hands and head as well. Jesus answered, *"Those who have had a bath need only to wash their feet."*

This picture reveals that while we are fully cleansed at salvation, we still walk through a fallen world and continually need the ongoing work of cleansing. Paul describes this tension in Romans 7:21–23: *"So I find this law at work: Although I want to do good, evil is right there with me. For in my inner being I delight in God's law; but I see another law at work in me, waging war against the law of my mind and making me a prisoner of the law of sin at work within me."*

Because of this reality, Paul could say, *"I die daily"* (1 Corinthians 15:31), and again, *"I have been crucified with Christ"* (Galatians 2:20). He exhorts believers in Colossians 3:5 to *"put to death, therefore, whatever belongs to your earthly nature: sexual immorality, impurity, lust, evil desires, and greed, which is idolatry."* In one sense, Christ crucified us with Himself; in another, we are called to actively crucify the old nature so that we may be found in Him, no longer living from our own life.

Inner healing is one of the ways we participate in this process. It is the invitation for Jesus to expose and remove whatever blocks the expression of His nature within us. Through inner healing, we allow Christ to complete our transformation by applying the power of His cross to every remaining area of our hearts.

Romans 8:18-19 says, *"I consider that our present sufferings are not worth comparing with the glory that will be revealed in us. The creation waits in eager expectation for [**the glory of**] the sons of God to be revealed."* **Glory** is "true nature or full essence" of a thing. Essence is the unique quality in nature that establishes your character. Truth is revealed in creation.

2 Peter 1:3-4 *"His **divine power** has given us everything we need for a godly life through our knowledge of him who called us by his own **glory** and goodness. Through these he has given us his very* *great and **precious promises**, so that through them you may participate in the **divine nature**, having escaped the corruption in the world caused by evil desires."*

A Major Tool for Sanctification

It is in the name of Jesus that demons are cast out but it is through the word of God, that strongholds are cast down.

2 Corinthians 10:3–6: *"For though we live in the world, we do not wage war as the world does. The weapons we fight with are not the weapons of this world, but have divine power to **demolish strongholds**. We demolish arguments and every proud obstacle that keeps people from knowing God, and we take captive every thought to make it obedient to Christ. And once your obedience is complete, we are ready to punish every act of disobedience."*

Strongholds are patterns of thought, and the word of God will demolish these strongholds, giving demons no place to return to. Romans 12:2 exhorts us, *"Do not conform to the **pattern of this world**, but be transformed by the renewing of your mind. Then you will be able to test and approve what God's will is—his good, pleasing and perfect will."*

Transformation is the process by which the Holy Spirit takes what is broken, distorted, or misaligned within us and redeems it, turning it into something that ultimately produces life and blessing. Inner healing does not erase our memories or rewrite our personal history. Instead, it brings truth into those moments so that the lies attached to them are removed. As a result, even our most painful experiences can become sacred ground, because we recognize that God was present, shaping us, teaching us, and preparing us to comfort and minister to others who have suffered in similar ways (see Hebrews 2:18).

Casting out a demon in the name of Jesus can occur in a moment. Dismantling strongholds, however, is a gradual process that happens through the renewing of the mind. We receive many requests for deliverance, but at times we must turn people away—not because we lack compassion, but because there is often a misunderstanding of what deliverance is, there is an effort to control the process, or a lack of connection to a local church or spiritual covering. In such cases, we encourage individuals to become rooted in a local ministry, because lasting freedom is cultivated through relationships and accountability—walking with a trusted partner or coach who can offer guidance and support along the way.

Application of Inner Healing

Inner healing takes place as we learn to listen to one another and invite the Holy Spirit to reveal those areas of our character that have not yet been brought to the cross—such as unforgiveness, bitterness, pride, heaviness, rejection, and similar issues. These unresolved traits often remain hidden until God lovingly exposes them so they can be surrendered and put to death.

Everything begins in seed form and rarely develops overnight. Through repeated exposure to negative experiences, especially in childhood, we often form coping mechanisms that once helped us survive but later cause us to think, act, and react in immature ways (see 1 Corinthians 13:11–12). When unforgiveness is present, bitter roots can spring back to life, defiling others and producing destructive consequences that, without godly counsel, we may not even understand.

Jesus illustrates this clearly in the Parable of the Unmerciful Servant (Matthew 18:21–35). After forgiving the servant's enormous debt, the king responds with anger when that same servant refuses to forgive another. Matthew 18:34 (NKJV) says the master *"delivered him to the torturers until he should pay all that was due to him."* The term "tormentors" (KJV) implies demonic oppression. When we refuse to forgive, we step outside the grace and mercy we ourselves received at the cross and place ourselves in a position of torment—until we choose to forgive. At any point, forgiveness restores grace and mercy. If unforgiveness continues, torment often gives way to bitterness, which in turn defiles many (Hebrews 12:15).

Our sense of reality is shaped by past experiences and the environment we continually allow to influence us. Over time, these experiences—and our reactions to them—form our perspective of truth. When unresolved pain is carried forward, it is often because we walked away believing a lie rather than embracing God's truth. That lie leaves a door open for the enemy to access our lives, causing us to live and respond as though past wounds are still present and active. Inner healing is one of the Lord's most powerful means of bringing these lingering issues to the cross, closing those doors, and leading us into lasting freedom.

1. Recognize:

Recognizing old emotions, patterns, family curses or heart "structures" that still need redemption is the first step in inner healing. This awareness invites us to examine our emotional responses. For example, when an offering is taken in church, what is the first emotion that rises within you? Do you feel taken advantage of? If so, that reaction often points back to a past experience where someone did exploit or misuse your trust. An unresolved wound like this can be used by the enemy to keep a person bound—often affecting areas such as provision, generosity, and freedom. Here are key factors to consider when performing inner healing:

SEVEN LANDING PADS OF THE ENEMY
(from *Emotionally Free,* by Rita Bennett)
      a. **Willful unrepentant sin, and habitual sin** – undealt with (1 John 1:6-7).
      b. **Involvement with cults and the occult** – the contract must be nullified - (Deuteronomy 18:9-14 - God's protective boundaries: do not cross).
      c. **Unhealed childhood trauma** (Mark 9:21).
- Abuse or accidental.
- My sin in response.

      d. **Unhealed sustained adult trauma.**
      e. **Generational bondage** – undealt with (Exodus 20:5-6).
- Involuntary sins.
- Ancestral sins.

      f. **Addiction** – alcohol, drugs, open the door to the enemy.
      g. **Abandonment** – physically or emotionally, especially childhood.

2. Repentance:

Once the lie has been identified, the next step is repentance, which means changing the way we think about the issue. Repentance requires a conscious decision to change for the right reasons—not merely for personal comfort, but for the sake of the Lord and for those around us who may be affected by our unresolved patterns. In repentance, we choose to place God's promise over our past pain and allow that promise to become the new lens through which we see life, replacing old interpretations with His truth.

3. Going to the Cross When it is Ripe:

The next step is praying aloud—asking for forgiveness and bringing to the cross whatever practices or patterns the Holy Spirit has brought to light (see Colossians 3:9–10). These patterns do not die easily. Both the person receiving healing and the prayer minister must stand firmly in Christ. True *ripeness* comes when we develop a deep hatred for sin and willingly let it go, choosing to bear the cost of change, whatever that cost may be. Ripeness also involves longing to become the good soil Jesus described—soil that receives the seed of His Word, holds fast to it, and produces fruit through perseverance.

Jesus warns in Mark 4:18–19 that the seed sown among thorns initially receives the Word, but the cares of this life, the deceitfulness of wealth, and the desire for other things choke it, leaving it unfruitful. Likewise, in Matthew 13:36–40, Jesus explains the parable of the weeds: the Son of Man sows good seed, the enemy sows weeds, and both grow together until the harvest, when final separation takes place. In both parables, the soil itself is capable of producing whatever is planted in it.

Becoming ripe, then, requires receiving enough love to stand, to confront what is false and to change. One of the most demanding aspects of inner-healing ministry is extending unconditional love again and again, until the fallow ground of a person's heart is broken up and becomes good soil (see Hosea 10:12).

In Matthew 13:24–30, Jesus speaks of the tares among the wheat. While people were sleeping, the enemy sowed tares among the wheat and left. Jesus' remedy is found in verse 30: *"Let both grow together until the harvest."* Wherever there is a counterfeit, there is also an original. Tares can only be uprooted when a person matures and is secure in the wheat— it is only then that separation can happen as the identity of a son/daughter are formed by the words of a loving Father.

Before beginning inner healing, create an atmosphere for the Holy Spirit to move by inviting Him in. Prayer counselor will read aloud and personalize Psalm 139 for the prayee as well as the Lord's Prayer in Matthew 6:9-15.

Psalm 139 says (verse 19-21 omitted), *"Lord, you know everything there is to know about _____. You perceive every movement of his/her heart and soul, and you understand his/her every thought before it even enters his/her mind. You are so intimately aware of him/her, Lord. You read his/her heart like an open book and you know all the words he/she is about to speak before he/she even starts a sentence! You know every step he/she will take before his/her journey even begins. You've gone into his/her future to prepare the way, and in kindness you follow behind him/her* **to spare him/her from the harm of his/her past.** *With your hand of love upon his/her life, you impart blessing to him/her. This is just too wonderful, deep, and incomprehensible! Your understanding of him/her brings them wonder and strength. Where could we go from your Spirit? Where could we run and hide from your face? If we go up to heaven, you're there! If we go down to the realm of the dead, you're there too! If we fly with wings into the shining dawn, you're there! If we fly into the radiant sunset, you're there waiting! Wherever we go, your hand will guide us; your strength will empower us. It's impossible to disappear from you or to ask the darkness to hide me, for your presence is everywhere, bringing light into his/her night. There is no such thing as darkness with you. The night, to you, is as bright as the day; there's no difference between the two. You formed _____ in his/her innermost being, shaping his/her delicate inside and his/her intricate outside, and wove him/her all together in his/her mother's womb. I thank you, God, for making _____ so mysteriously complex! Everything you do is marvelously breathtaking. It simply amazes us to think about it! How thoroughly you know _____, Lord! You even formed every bone in his/her body when you created him/her in the secret place, carefully, skillfully shaping him/her from nothing to something. You saw who you created _____ to be before he/she became into being! Before they ever saw the light of day, the number of days you planned for him/her were already recorded in your book. Every single moment you are thinking of him/her! How precious and wonderful to consider that you cherish him/her constantly in your every thought! O God, your desires toward _____ are more than the grains of sand on every shore! When I awake each morning, you're still with him/her... God, we invite your searching gaze into _____'s heart. Examine him/her through and through; find out everything that may be hidden within him/her. Put him/her to the test and sift through all his/her anxious cares. See if there is any path of pain he/she is walking on, and lead him/her back to your glorious, everlasting ways— the path that brings him/her back to you, in Jesus' name."*

State out loud Matthew 6:9-15 *"Our Father, who is in heaven, hallowed be your name. Your Kingdom come, Your will be done, on earth as it is in heaven. Give us this day our daily bread. And forgive us our debts, as we have forgiven our debtors (letting go of both the wrong and the resentment). And do not lead us into temptation, but deliver us from evil. (For Yours is the kingdom and the power and the glory forever. Amen)."*

Have the prayee confess, "Father, I come to you, in the name of Jesus, and I yield my will to you. I give You permission to go to any level within me, to heal me, to cleanse me and to restore me according to Your truth. To the best of my ability I invite you to be my Lord, unconditionally. Please be the Lord of my subconscious, as well as my conscious mind. I renounce every false teaching and attitude, and ask you to cleanse and protect me with Jesus' blood. I cast down every wrong thought, imagination, and everything that exalts itself against the knowledge of God, and I bring every thought captive to the Lord Jesus Christ (2 Cor 10:5 Personalized from, Rita Bennett, *Emotionally Free.*)

    a. **Confess the lie/truth:** First, make sure the prayee has their eyes closed throughout the entire session. Confession is the key to expose darkness and remove its power from a believer's life. James 5:16 AMP says, *"Therefore, confess your sins to one another (your offenses), and pray for one another, that you may be healed and restored. The heartfelt and persistent prayer of a righteous man (believer) can accomplish much [when put into action and made effective by God—it is dynamic and can have tremendous power]."*

Evil only has power in darkness. When we confess the issues of our heart that have been hidden in darkness, a word of knowledge is released by a Prayer Counselor and evil is dislodged from darkness and brought into the light where it is rendered void of any power. Start from the most recent wound they can recall, and work back toward childhood. Ask for the Holy Spirit to help. If they cannot pinpoint the wound, identify the strongest and repetitious negative emotion that they feel. Find out when this happened in their life. Have the prayee walk you through the scene as far as what happened. The prayer counselor should write everything down. Have prayee tell you how they felt (abandoned, hopeless, angry, etc.). Prayer Counselor to write all of the emotions down. Ask the Holy Spirit if there is anything else He desires to show the prayee, and write it down. During prayer, keep directing the prayee to Jesus, and away from yourself. Once you have the emotions written out, you will later use this to identify the "strongman" or main negative spirit over the emotions. You will go after these spirits in the deliverance portion of their breakthrough.

    b. **Hear from Jesus to Discover the Truth**: Ask the Holy Spirit to show them where Jesus is in the situation as well as what He may have done or said. This is where the prayee receives insights, understandings, affirmations or replacement of error with truth. Or Ask the Holy Spirit to be able to see the people and circumstance through the eyes of Jesus (pause and wait).

    c. **Forgiveness:** Lead prayee into closing doors to the admission of spirits. Take them through forgiveness from the emotions of the past. In the following verbal release, in a prayerful attitude, have the prayee forgive and speak forgiveness from the time of the memory. Remember, God will not command you to do anything without supplying you with the necessary grace to do it (2 Corinthians 9:8, Philippians 4:13). The memory tape has rolled back and they are there emotionally. Have the prayee follow the prayer counselor phrase by phrase in the first-person mode, then have them fill in where needed.

    i. **Speaking Forgiveness:** (say out loud)

"Through Jesus, I forgive _____ for _____. I won't hold this against you any longer. Even though my flesh wants vengeance, I know it is Your will that I forgive to be released from demonic entanglements and attachments. Father, in the same manner that you have forgiven me of all my offenses, I choose now to forgive my offender. I release _____ into your hands. I give up every "right" to harbor resentment against them. I also ask for forgiveness for receiving the lie and I ask for forgiveness for feeling _____ (be specific). You said you would never leave me nor forsake me; I am your son/daughter and nothing can separate me from your love. I close the doors to the wounds of my past and I plead the blood of Jesus over them as a wall of separation between us. Thank you, Jesus, that your blood has cleansed me from all sins. Help me to bring my emotions into my alignment with my choice to forgive and to live a life that will honor you, in Jesus' name."

    d. **Renounce:** Renounce all sins or spirits involved, in the name of Jesus. Renunciation is audible and firm. This is not a prayer to God. **It is spoken to the negative spirit involved**, who is an enemy opposed to the will of God for your life. This is a prayer of **Command** to an enemy, not a petition to God.

    e. **Prayer Counselor to Close the Door:** State (while maintaining eye contact), "Father, I come to you in the name of Jesus and I bind the spirit of _____ and its demons and I break its hold over _____ (person's name) so that when they are cast out, they will not come back. I break the power of every curse that they have released over someone's life or that they have received in their hearts. In the name of Jesus, I command you to loose them and let them go. I close every door that you have used to access their heart and life and I plead the blood of Jesus over it as a wall of separation between you. Holy

Spirit, come into their life and fill every place in their heart that was once occupied and influenced by the enemy."

Chapter 8 – Why Deliverance?

In 2018, the Holy Spirit began speaking to me about going deeper in the area of deliverance. After personally experiencing freedom through this ministry, the Lord instructed me not only to teach on the subject, but also to demonstrate it. As a Christian man and leader, I have discovered that pastors and leaders often do not struggle as much with the concept of deliverance as they do with the level of transparency it requires.

Trust is built most quickly in areas where wounds exist, especially when leaders are willing to be transparent—because transparency invites transparency. True transparency is a mark of maturity. Maturity is seen when a leader can pick up trash in the parking lot before a service without feeling that it diminishes their position or authority. It is also seen when a leader is willing to invite others into his or her heart through vulnerability.

You cannot freely give what you have not first received and possess. And you cannot ask people to walk in a level of grace that you yourself are not walking in. This principle is clearly illustrated in the account of the seven sons of Sceva in Acts 19:14–17. If parents—both natural and spiritual—are called to raise children in the way they should go, then we have no right to demand from them something that is not first evident in our own lives first (Proverbs 22:6). When a parent calls me and says their child needs deliverance, my first question is, "Where did it come from?" A parent's victory often becomes a child's freedom, just as a parent's unresolved issues can become a child's bondage.

When the Lord called me to teach on the subject of deliverance, He also warned me that persecution would follow. One fellow pastor—let's call him Larry— strongly disagreed with our theology regarding Christians being demonized. One Sunday, a young man came to our church who had been in and out of our youth ministry for several years. We had not seen him in a couple of weeks, and I immediately sensed that something about him had changed. As I approached him, I saw yellow eyes behind his eyes. He immediately looked down, and I went to Pastor Larry and said, "That kid has a demon." Larry responded, "I talked to him earlier and he seems fine to me. He doesn't have a demon."

I immediately went to the head usher, pointed the young man out, and said, "Keep an eye on him. When worship starts, he may manifest." The usher looked at me strangely as this was not a normal request, but he agreed.

As soon as worship began, the young man growled and barked like a dog, ran to the front of the church, and began choking the senior pastor. He was quickly removed from the service, and from that moment on, our church protocol changed. The senior pastor's wife later said to me, "If they won't listen to you, I will. If you ever see something like that again, please tell me." Since then, I have informed her when demonized individuals, Satanists, or witches have entered our services, and I have helped our leadership and usher team establish clear protocols for handling such situations.

On another occasion, my wife and I along with our altar team were invited to serve at a youth crusade where four churches had come together and approximately 1,600 students from various churches were in attendance. We were asked to oversee the altar ministry at this event. After the minister preached and opened the altar for prayer, several young people began to fall to the ground, screaming, kicking, and vomiting.

We were called over to help a young woman who was curled up in a fetal position, kicking her legs and covering her ears. I immediately recognized that she was reliving a traumatic experience. Her youth pastor, a young man, had laid his hands on her to pray. As I approached, the Holy Spirit spoke clearly to me and said, "She was raped." I told the youth pastor to remove his hands, and he immediately did so. I then asked my wife, Kristen, along with the women from our altar team, to take the young woman to the church office as we wanted to save her dignity. With the permission of the event leadership, they ministered the deliverance and care she needed in a private and safe setting.

While the women were ministering to her in the back room, I instructed the ushers to bring the youth pastor to me. When he saw the young woman on the couch, still kicking and screaming, I asked him, "What do you think is causing this?" He responded, "You know what it is." I replied, "I do, but I want to hear you say it." He said nothing further.

After the conference, the senior leadership called me in to discuss what had happened. Despite what they had witnessed, they were dismissive of the deliverance and stood firmly by their belief that believers cannot be demonized.

Deliverance is freedom from the molestation of the enemy. If you pray for enough people, it is only a matter of time before you encounter someone who is demonized. As we touched on in earlier chapters, we use the term *demonized* rather than *possessed* because the enemy does not own the person—God does. To be demonized means that a believer has unintentionally given the enemy access to an area of the heart through a carnal coping mechanism that eventually becomes a demonic stronghold. The enemy is a tenant, not an owner. These strongholds can form through unforgiveness, unhealthy soul ties, sexual trauma such as rape, generational curses, witchcraft, and other open doors.

Steps for Deliverance

At times, while praying for the sick, it becomes clear that unresolved unforgiveness is hindering the person's healing. In these moments, it is often best to gently lead them in a short, simple prayer of forgiveness for the individual or individuals involved. Have them repent for their unforgiveness, ask the Lord for forgiveness, and then verbally renounce the spirits of unforgiveness, bitterness, and anger. After this, you, as the minister, break the power of those spirits and command them to leave. This process can be done quietly and respectfully, without extended interviewing or drawing unnecessary attention.

In many situations, a person's sickness is connected to an afflicting or tormenting spirit—such as a spirit of pain, infirmity, or stiffness. These spirits can often be expelled with a direct command. When prayers are kept short and accompanied by brief check-ins with the person, it becomes easier to discern the effectiveness of speaking a word of authority and casting the spirit out.

In cases involving chronic or severe conditions—such as diabetes, cancer, or long-standing illness—there may be a "strongman" associated with the sickness. When this is the case, ministry may require more time. It often involves identifying and closing the open door that gave the enemy access before commanding the spirit to leave.

10-Step Prayer Model for Deliverance

When conducting a deliverance session, this 10-step prayer model acts as a guide to navigate setting your church members free. It works ideally after walking them through inner healing so that they are now open to receive freedom. It is often best received when two ministers of the same gender pray with the person, helping them feel safe, open, and fully at ease.

STEP 1: Give the Individual Priority

Your posture in ministry should be loving, not militant. The focus must be far more on love, compassion, and acceptance for the person you are praying for than on any hostility toward the demon. When you minister from this place, the "prayee" knows you are on their side. This builds trust and invites them to partner with you in contending for their freedom.

Be encouraging and intentional about restoring hope. Continually emphasize that Jesus is able and willing to set them free. Do not magnify the power of the enemy; any demonic power is already subject to the authority of Jesus' name.

Keep in mind that the person you are praying for may have been in bondage for years and may have received many prayers that did not bring full breakthrough. As a result, their hope may be diminished. Your role is to rebuild that hope. Encourage them to approach this moment as if it were the first time they are receiving prayer for this issue, allowing their expectations to be renewed and aligned with faith.

STEP 2: Dealing with a Manifestation

If a spirit manifests during ministry, immediately take authority and command it to be quiet and submit in the name of Jesus. Use a clear, firm command such as, "Be quiet, in Jesus' name." Repeat the command as needed until the spirit comes under submission. You may need to say it multiple times, but it will submit. Remember, there is no volume in the spirit realm. Speak firmly, not loudly. A stern, authoritative tone is sufficient—there is no need to shout. Demons seek attention, and we do not give them what they want. If the person receiving prayer is aware of what is happening, calmly explain that you are speaking to the spirit manifesting and not to them.

If you are performing this in a church setting (i.e. at the altar) and others begin to gather while you are quieting the spirit, ask them not to touch the person and not to speak or pray aloud. Loud prayers and multiple voices can agitate the situation and create confusion, which is counterproductive. If the manifestation continues and there is no immediate change, discreetly and gently remove the person from the service to a private room where you can minister with focus and respect.

The first priority in deliverance is protecting the dignity of the individual. In our church, ushers are trained to escort individuals needing deliverance to a designated room. Because demons seek to disrupt public gatherings, we lovingly and quickly obtain permission to move the person to a private space where they can receive undivided attention and ministry.

When ministering as a team, one person leads the deliverance. Everyone else stands aside quietly in intercession, without touching or speaking, unless they sense they have a word from the Holy Spirit. If someone does step forward to share, the leader simply changes places with them so order and authority are maintained.

If a demon manifests in an area where the prayer counselor does not have victory, that counselor should immediately ask for a replacement. This is not a matter of condemnation. You cannot freely give what you do not possess, and the goal is always the freedom of the person receiving ministry. The most qualified minister should lead so the individual can be helped effectively and safely.

STEP 3: Establish and Maintain Communication with the Prayee

You must be able to communicate with the person receiving ministry, because their cooperation is essential for deliverance to be effective. Periodically check in by asking whether they can hear you, whether their eyes are open or closed. Maintaining clear communication helps keep the person present and engaged in the process.

At times, maintaining that connection may require additional commands for the spirit to submit. The person may lower their head, close their eyes, or allow their eyes to wander. Gently but firmly instruct them to lift their head, open their eyes, and look at you. If you are unsure whether they can hear you, simply ask and wait for a response.

If the person stands up or begins moving around, take authority out loud over the spirit—often an attempt at escapism—and instruct the person to return and sit down. At times, a spirit may attempt to intimidate by suggesting you lack the faith or authority to drive it out. Do not engage or retreat. Continue pressing forward in confidence and obedience.

Jude 1:6 reminds us that even angels who abandoned their assigned authority are restrained by God until judgment. In the same way, all demonic powers remain subject to the authority of Jesus Christ, and you are to minister from that place of confidence and order.

STEP 4: Ask the Prayee What He/She Wants to Be Free From

In a crusade setting, ask the person receiving ministry what they want to be free from. If they are unsure, ask what the speaker was praying or saying at the time the manifestation began. You may also ask whether there are any persistent habits, behaviors, or patterns they have been unable to overcome despite repeated effort.

In a private ministry setting, the person seeking prayer will usually be aware of the bondages they desire freedom from. Often this information has already been shared with the minister through a questionnaire or prior conversation.

If a spirit manifests but the person does not want ministry, honor their decision. Likewise, if they choose to leave after only partial ministry, allow them to do so. Never attempt to restrain someone or minister to them against their will.

Some individuals want relief from the compulsive aspect of a behavior—such as smoking, anger, or pornography—without addressing the underlying root or surrendering the behavior itself (see Matthew 13:30, "Let both grow together"). Continuing to engage in the activity that opened the door will reopen it, and the bondage will return.

Relationship is essential. If, after conversation, it becomes clear that the person does not want deliverance, intends to continue in their current lifestyle, or is otherwise not ready for ministry, pray for them, bless them, and encourage them to return when they are ready. Do not pray for deliverance in such cases.

STEP 5: Make Sure the Prayee Has Accepted Jesus as His Lord and Savior

Remember, it is our authority that helps initiate freedom, but it is their authority—under Jesus as Lord and the ongoing work of the Holy Spirit in their lives—that sustains that freedom. This is why deliverance is often referred to as "the children's bread." A person is in need of deliverance when there are areas of their soul or life that have not yet been fully redeemed by the cross of Jesus.

STEP 6: Interview to Discover the Event or Events, or the Relationship Situations that Have Led to His Bondage(s) and/or Physical Condition

1. The purpose is to discover where forgiveness is required and where healing, repentance and breaking of bondages are needed.

2. Find all open doors (used if not taking them through a complete inner healing session prior to deliverance). If there is no obvious place to start, begin with parental relationships then move to other relationships closest to him/her. You may want to ask questions as to what was going on when this started, such as, "Are your parents divorced or separated? Were you a planned pregnancy? Any trauma during the pregnancy or childbirth? Any trauma as a child?" Finding out when the trauma happened would be your starting point. We have to go back from there as oftentimes what they remember was not the starting point but a compounding issue from the original trauma. Be thorough, don't rush. Have them close their eyes and ask the Holy Spirit to show them the root cause. Have them tell you what comes to mind or what they see.

3. Keep a note of the manifestations or spirits, emotions and the strongmen (See *Strongman* by Jerry Roberson).

4. Do they hear voices in their head? Do they feel tormented?

5. Consider a curse if the person has difficulty in any area of life. A curse is a repetitious cycle of failure such as persistent difficulty in life, inability to keep a job, accident prone, addiction, worthlessness, repeated illnesses, etc.

6. Trauma and fear are a common entry point for many different spirits and illnesses.

STEP 7: Close The Doors

1. Close the doors to the admission of spirits – Renounce any sin and forgive others, God and self:

    a. Forgive whoever caused the hurt and led them into wrong conduct.

    b. Forgive themself for believing the lie and empowering the liar.

    c. Repent and ask for forgiveness of specific sins (1 John 1:9).

    d. Lead the prayee to renounce all sins or spirits involved. This is not a prayer or petition to God. It is a command to the enemy that is audible and firm, and spoken to the spirit(s) involved. The prayer counselor should lead them by saying, "Repeat after me..." and guide them to renounce the spirits involved.

    e. Renounce the inner vows that opened the door:

        i. The prayer counselor should break the yoke of bondage and the power of any spirit. "In the name of Jesus, I break the power of the spirit(s) of _____ over (person's name). I break every tie, entanglement and attachment connecting you to their life, and I plead the blood of Jesus as a wall of separation between you."

      ii.   Break the tie to the person/thing that the curse is tied to. "In the name of Jesus, I break the power of every curse over (person's name) from _____ (family member, critical words, rejection, etc.) and I plead the blood of Jesus as a wall of separation between you."

STEP 8: Cast Out

      1.   When the doors are closed, make sure the prayee primes the pump by taking deep breaths. Spirits are like air that you expel and it makes it easier for releasing any demon. Sometimes a person may cough or yawn in this process without coaching. While the prayer counselor is commanding the spirits to leave, have the prayee breathe out. When all doors are closed, the spirits will leave quickly and quietly.

          a.   Automatically look for infirmity and cast it out.

            i.   Pray again for healing.

            ii.   Re-interview to see how they feel or if the pain/problem still exists.

      2. If the spirits do not leave, go back to Step 1 or Deliverance and re-interview.

STEP 9: Praise and Thank Jesus for Deliverance

If the prayee cannot thank Jesus or if there is further demonic manifestation when he/she does thank Jesus, it is a sign that there are more doors to be closed and more spirits to be expelled. Ask the Holy Spirit for His help and go back through Step 6 and 7 as indicated.

STEP 10: Holy Spirit Infilling

      1.   Ask the Holy Spirit to sweep through the person's heart and reveal anything that is still there. Cast it out.

      2.   Ask the Holy Spirit to fill the prayee in every place the enemy once influenced and occupied.

*The 10 steps are followed in a session where, typically, the minister does not know the host person intimately. For example, where the minister knows the prayee is a believer and really wants to be set free, step 5 (accepting Jesus) would be omitted. If there is no manifestation during the ministry, step 2 and 3 would be omitted.

Post-Deliverance Ministry

Just because a person has been set free from demons does not mean their habits will automatically change. This is where encouragement is essential. They need to be asked what environments they are re-entering, and whether those environments will support and protect their freedom. It is also important to emphasize the necessity of daily quiet time and prayer, regular time in the Word, and being firmly planted in a local church community.

Post-Session Prayer to Deslime

This is an important step for ministers to understand. When a demon is cast out of a person or a place, it seeks to land elsewhere. We once conducted a deliverance session in our home and forgot to deslime afterward. That night, Kristen woke up to a spirit of fear standing over her, attempting to stab her. She immediately commanded it to leave and then deslimed our home. Any place where deliverance occurs, and anyone involved in the ministry, needs to be deslimed to ensure that no lingering spiritual residue remains.

Prayer: *"Lord Jesus, I plead the blood of Jesus over my life and over the lives of my family. I ask that you cleanse me with your blood and I hereby cancel any assignment of hell or its agents, and release the assignments of heaven over our lives. Lord Jesus, bless me and protect me by keeping my mind pure. Help me to guard my emotions against anything that would come against my knowledge of You. Protect my body from sickness and disease and bless those who would curse me, in Jesus' name."*

Guidelines for Deliverance

Your context and demographic always shape how deliverance is practiced. You operate under the authority of the ministry and within the culture and expectations of the region you are serving. When I was in Liberia, Africa, we prayed for the sick, and when pastors noticed a demonized person manifesting in the crowd, they would bring that person forward for ministry. Often the individual would fall to the ground, hissing and slithering like a snake. The pastors would deliver those who came to the crusade by simply commanding the demon to come out. Once free, the individuals filled out contact cards, attended church the following Sunday, and were connected to newcomer classes.

We do not believe in repeatedly commanding a spirit to leave, as that approach exhausts everyone involved. In those situations, you are contending not only with the will of the enemy but also with the will of the person receiving ministry. Our goal is to bring the person into agreement with God's will so that we can partner with them and coach them toward freedom. When the person's will aligns with God's will, deliverance becomes far more effective. That said, in Liberia this was the established method, and we honored their way of doing ministry.

While praying for the sick in Brazil, a man came to the altar with schizophrenia. Before ministering to him, I informed the leadership of his condition and asked for permission to proceed, since deliverance might be required and a demon could manifest. The leadership approved, so I prayed, kept the deliverance very gentle, and afterward connected the man with a leader in their ministry for follow-up.

In our ministry in Seattle, many people walk into our church specifically asking for deliverance. We also receive calls from people who say they need help because they believe they have a demon. We never question whether Jesus can set someone free. Our concern is whether the person can sustain their freedom.

Jesus warned about this reality in Matthew 12:43–45:

"When an evil spirit leaves a person, it goes into the desert, seeking rest but finding none. Then it says, 'I will return to the person I came from.' So it returns and finds its former home empty, swept, and in order. Then it finds seven other spirits more evil than itself, and they all enter and live there. And so that person is worse off than before."

Because of this, when someone goes through deliverance in our ministry, they are assigned a partner or coach for the first thirty days to help them walk out their freedom successfully. If a person has no intention of being planted in a church, we will not pray for their deliverance. We have seen people's conditions worsen when deliverance was done prematurely, improperly, or left them without any support or follow-up. We have had to minister to individuals who were harmed by ineffective deliverance sessions in other churches. If someone wants us to coach them through deliverance, they must be willing to follow that guidance or seek another coach.

Psalm 92:13 says, *"Those who are planted in the house of the Lord shall flourish in the courts of our God."* We believe that when someone plants themselves in a spirit filled church, freedom begins to work in their life naturally. After a person has been with us for a few months, and strongholds still need to be addressed, we provide suggested reading materials and ask them to complete some paperwork before proceeding with deliverance. We will explore this process further in the next chapter.

Chapter 9 – Spiritual Housecleaning

The Fall of Adam Defiled Humanity and the Land

God is in charge of Heaven and Earth. In Genesis 1:26, God had given mankind spiritual authority (dominion) over the whole of the earth. He not only gave Adam spiritual authority, but commissioned mankind to steward the earth and all its inhabitants (Ps 115:16). Through the Fall, whatever man had been given authority over was submitted to the god of this world (Satan). Because God gave Adam "freewill" to choose, He could do very little when Adam decided to give the keys of authority to the planet over to Satan.

In Genesis 3:17-19 God said to Adam, *"Because you listened to your wife and ate fruit from the tree about which I commanded you, 'You must not eat from it,' Cursed is the ground because of you; through painful toil you will eat food from it all the days of your life. It will produce thorns and thistles for you, and you will eat the plants of the field. By the sweat of your brow you will eat your food until you return to the ground, since from it you were taken; for dust you are and to dust you will return."*

This single act of disobedience brought a curse upon the earth and all its inhabitants, rendering creation unholy under Satan's spiritual influence. Because Satan is an "unclean spirit," sin gave him legal access to humanity and to what belonged to them—health, land, buildings, possessions, and more. As a result, contact with people or their possessions could knowingly or unknowingly expose others to the influence of the demonic powers attached to them. In the same way that contact with a leper resulted in leprosy regardless of one's awareness, exposure to a curse carried real consequences whether understood or not.

The Fall fundamentally altered humanity. Spiritual death came first, and physical death followed. The effects were not limited to mankind alone; the land entrusted to humanity was also transformed. Before the Fall, Adam needed only to sow in order to reap. Afterward, he was required to labor and struggle to produce a harvest, because what he once ruled now resisted him and his descendants. The ground had to be continually cultivated, or it would return to its fallen condition.

Scripture tells us how sin defiles the land and its consequences for us. Defiled land is mentioned in the Old Testament 11 times (see Lev 11:44; 18:25, 27-28; Num 35:34; Deut. 24:4: Jer. 2:7; Ezek. 22:4; 33:26; 36:17-18). Leviticus 18:24-25 says, *"Do not defile yourselves in any of these ways, because this is how the nations that I am going to drive out before you became defiled. Even the land was defiled; so I punished it for its sin, and the land vomited out its inhabitants."*

The Hebrew word for "defiled" is translated as *tame*, which means "to be foul or unclean," especially in a ceremonial or moral sense. When a land is defiled, it is spiritually polluted by sin, idols, broken covenants, sexual perversion and the shedding of innocent blood. Because of human sin, *"we are conscious that all living things are weeping and sorrowing together in pain until now"* (Romans 8:22). As carcasses attract the vultures of the air, defiled land attracts spiritual wickedness. Humanity is the link that connects the realm of the spirit to the land.

Spiritual Deposits

While no one fully understands how spiritual deposits or imprints are left in a place, we do know that they exist and that their effects can be observed. Advances in technology called Kirlian photography have allowed researchers to photograph energy fields that remain in a location after a person has been there, particularly when that person has experienced intense stress. Scientists have also noted that plants can respond to sensory impressions in their environment. When a plant is damaged, it releases chemicals that warn nearby plants and neighboring plants then alter their chemistry defensively within seconds to minutes. Stone Tape Theory states that certain stones can record traumatic events and later release them under certain conditions.

Scripture affirms this reality. After Cain murdered his brother Abel, God said, *"The voice of your brother's blood is crying out to Me from the ground"* (Genesis 4:10). Because of this act, Cain was told that the ground would no longer yield its strength to him (Genesis 4:11–12). Isaiah 33:8–9 speaks of the land and trees suffering because of human sin, and Revelation 18:2–3 indicates that demonic powers are drawn not only to people who persist in sin, but also to places where sin has been practiced. Just as music can be imprinted onto records or CDs, it follows that emotions and events can be imprinted onto locations or objects in ways that people can sense and even come under the influence of.

On one occasion, my family and I stayed at a hotel during a vacation. After our first night, we went to breakfast and realized that every member of our family had experienced a nightmare the previous night. I sensed that there was a spiritual deposit in the room attempting to affect us. I left breakfast early, returned to the room alone, and prayed. I laid my hands on the doorframes and walls and declared that the blood of Jesus cleanse the room and establish a clear boundary between blessing and curse. I proclaimed that because we are blessed by God, the room was blessed as well, and I commanded every unclean spirit to leave immediately. For the rest of our stay, no one experienced another nightmare.

Several years later, our church was given a church building by another ministry. During a service, as the pastor preached and spoke the name "Jesus," a man repeatedly responded out loud with "Yahweh." This happened multiple times. I asked him to stop, but when he continued, I asked him to move to the back of the church. Even there, he persisted, speaking out loudly and disrupting both the senior pastor and the congregation. After several corrections, I ultimately asked him to leave.

A few months later, another individual attended a service and exhibited the same behavior. I responded in the same way, and that person also had to leave. Then, months later again, the same thing happened with yet another individual, with the same outcome.

Whenever we minister deliverance out of our own home, we make it a practice to "deslime" both ourselves and our house, praying that any spiritual residue connected to what has been confronted and driven out does not remain. Reflecting on these repeated incidents in the church, I realized an important oversight: while we were addressing individuals, we were not addressing the spiritual environment of the inherited building itself. When the same spirit is confronted and driven out, but later returns through someone else under its influence, it becomes necessary to cleanse the space as well. This led me to ask an important question—how often do we intentionally pray over and cleanse our local churches after repeated spiritual conflicts?

Obedience is Worship and Transfers Ownership

Genesis 1:1-2 says, *"When Abram was ninety-nine years old, the Lord appeared to him and said, 'I am El-Shaddai—God Almighty. Serve me faithfully and live a blameless life. I will make a covenant with you, by which I will guarantee to give you countless descendants.'"* Abram chose to obey God and made a covenant with God to obey Him. It was through this covenant that a new bloodline was created and the nation of Israel was birthed. Not only was a new bloodline created, but through obedience to God, Abraham and his descendants exercised a higher spiritual authority than that which was given to Satan. When we choose to walk in fellowship and obedience to God, we experience the blessing, protection and freedom Jesus provided for us on the cross.

Since the Garden, God has granted humanity free will, as character is formed through choice. It is through this freedom that Satan seeks to reassert his influence... tempting humanity to remain enslaved through misplaced obedience and worship. When God's people fail to choose Him or to steward what He set apart for them, they default to their fallen, carnal nature. In doing so, they place themselves back under the curse by submitting to the enemy's influence. They empower what is inferior over what is superior and become enslaved to the one they choose to obey.

Further evidence of what happened to the earth and its kingdoms of the world after the Fall was displayed by Satan when he tempted Jesus in the wilderness. Luke 4:5-7 says, *"The devil led him up to a high place and showed him in an instant all the kingdoms of the world. And he said to him, 'I will give you all their authority and splendor; it has been given to me, □and I can give it to anyone I want to. □□If you worship me, it will all be yours.'"*

Jesus did not dispute Satan's claim that the kingdoms of the world had been placed under his control. Satan tied obedience to worship, because obedience is worship, and worship transfers authority. Had Jesus obeyed Satan, He would have received delegated power, but only by placing Himself under Satan's rule—binding humanity to that dominion forever. In the same way, when we obey Satan, we are worshiping him and granting him influence over our lives. What may feel like gaining control is, in reality, surrendering it; we give the enemy permission to rule where obedience is misplaced.

How did Jesus defeat Satan? He took up His cross and fully embraced His divine purpose. Through the cross, He fulfilled His assignment, exercised Kingdom authority, and destroyed the works of the enemy (Galatians 3:13–14; 1 John 3:8). By choosing obedience to God and completing His mission through sacrificial obedience, Jesus walked in unlimited access to God's grace, wisdom, and power—for Himself and for us. When we choose Jesus, we become children of God (John 1:12), and as children, we too are called to take up our cross (Matthew 16:24). Carrying our cross positions us to live in higher Kingdom authority, placing Satan and the curse beneath our feet.

Consecrating Ourselves Comes First

Before we cleanse anything else, we must first cleanse ourselves. In 2 Chronicles 29, after Hezekiah became king, he was called to purify the Temple. Yet before the Temple and its objects could be cleansed, the priests themselves had to be consecrated. They needed to be free from every influence of the enemy so that the Temple and its furnishings could be made ritually clean. It is through human sin or blessing that the spiritual realm is given access to connect with the land.

Each day, we live and work within the world's system and receive provision through it. When Adam fell, he obeyed Satan and disobeyed God. Although Jesus redeemed humanity from the curse of the law, Scripture still refers to Satan as "the god of this world" (2 Corinthians 4:4), meaning he continues to influence the world's systems. We participate in these systems daily—investing our time and energy to be productive members of society and to meet our financial responsibilities. Most of us also work under human authority (Romans 13:1–2).

If obedience is worship, and we become servants to the one we obey, how do we remain consecrated to God while functioning within a fallen system? Scripture provides the answer. Titus 3:1–2 instructs us to be subject to rulers and authorities and to be ready for every good work, while Colossians 3:23 reminds us to work with all our heart as unto the Lord, not for human masters. By maintaining our obedience to God in attitude, motive, and action, we remain consecrated to Him even as we operate within the world's system.

When we receive money from the world's system in exchange for our time and labor, that money must be consecrated to God. The biblical meaning of consecrating finances is by way of tithing. A tithe—one tenth—represents the whole and restores honor in our relationship with God by setting it apart before the Lord, placing it under His authority and protection, so the devourer cannot consume the seed sown in your field (Matthew 13:4, 19).

The tithe consecrates your "land," bringing it under God's covering so that it produces fruit through blessing rather than through the curse and its system of toil (Malachi 3:11). In this way, the tithe restores your land to God's original intention, reflecting the order of the Garden before the fall. When you sow in obedience, you place yourself under God's blessing, enabling you to reap without resistance from the land or interference from the devourer empowered by the fall. When you fail to sow, however, you allow Satan to reassert influence through toil— and toil produces delay, because it makes you dependent on time rather than on God's provision.

Spiritual Deposits in the Land

After Moses led Israel out of Egypt, the people were given the opportunity to walk in the blessing of God (Deuteronomy 28:1–14). This blessing reasserted Kingdom authority over the curse by positioning

Israel *"high above all the nations of the earth"* (Deuteronomy 28:1). The blessing was not limited to their physical or emotional well-being; it also extended to the land they were called to possess and steward.

Moses was instructed to remove his sandals because the ground on which he stood was holy—made holy by the presence of the living God (Exodus 3:5). In a similar way, Jesus washed the disciples' feet, acknowledging that their feet had been contaminated by unconsecrated ground. Obedience to God, in partnership with His presence, brings cleansing to all things (John 13). Scripture commands us to be holy as God is holy (Leviticus 19:2; 1 Peter 1:16). We do this by consecrating ourselves (Leviticus 20:7), and we consecrate ourselves by living as obedient children (1 Peter 1:14).

2 Chronicles 7:14 says, *"If my people, who are called by my name, will humble themselves and pray and seek my face and turn from their wicked ways, then I will hear from heaven, and I will forgive their sin and will heal their land."*

We do not always understand how spiritual deposits are left behind in a place. What we do know is that when spiritual authority is not maintained, that land set apart by God and redeemed through Christ, can be forfeited to the enemy. Often, satanists do not establish themselves in an area because of its natural beauty or resources, but because they perceive an existing spiritual deposit of evil in the land. For example, a recent large gathering of Satanists took place in Old Town Scottsdale, Arizona. One must ask whether this was merely because of the climate, or whether the land itself had already been spiritually defiled to draw them in.

Scripture gives us a parallel in Lot's choice of land. He selected a region that appeared prosperous like Eden and Egypt, yet he failed to discern the wickedness of the people who inhabited it. While intercession can sometimes bring temporary victory by driving such groups out, that victory may be short-lived if the underlying deposits of sin in the land are not addressed. Without repentance and consecration, the very conditions that allowed evil and demonic strongholds to take root remain in place.

Hosea 4:6 declares, *"My people are destroyed for lack of knowledge."* When we do not understand how to confront evil, we often minimize or dismiss it, leaving ourselves vulnerable to its influence. Just as individuals are forgiven, cleansed, and healed through repentance, Scripture teaches that land can also be cleansed and restored in the same way. The Bible is clear that sin defiles the land, hinders it from yielding its blessing, and can even make it a dwelling place for demons. Yet it is equally clear that repentance has the power to restore the land to its original state of blessing.

Spiritual Deposits in Buildings or Homes

After the period of apostasy, the priests were required not only to cleanse themselves ritually, but also to purify every object in the Temple. Each item had to be freed from any spiritual influence that had become attached to it through defilement. Those involved in occult practices understand the significance of this principle. They often place great value on objects that were once used for Christian worship and then repurposed for pagan or occult use, believing that the misuse of formerly consecrated items can carry greater demonic influence than objects that were never set apart to God.

We once had a man attend our church who brought and blew a shofar. A shofar is a ritual instrument made from a ram's horn and was historically used to mark sacred moments such as the Sabbath, the new moon, or the anointing of a king. Each time the shofar was blown during worship or at the altar, a noticeable sense of oppression filled the room. Knowing that one of the shofar's purposes is to proclaim the anointing of a king, I discerned that if oppression followed its sounding, the instrument itself had likely been previously used in an occult context. Each blast seemed to invite an unclean influence rather than the presence of God. Because I was leading the service that day, I instructed the ushers to prevent it from being sounded again. The man's immediate reaction was to protect the instrument from being taken, and he was then removed from the altar area.

When God gave Moses instructions for dedicating the Tent of the Lord's Presence, He said, *"Dedicate the Tent and all its equipment by anointing it with the sacred oil, and it will be holy"* (Exodus 40:9). As noted earlier, we live in a fallen world where, for a time, everything lies under the influence of the god of this world.

Before consecration, even the materials used to build the tent and its furnishings were subject to the enemy's influence. It was the act of consecration that set them apart for holy use.

When the Lord opens the eyes of His servants to discern the past of a place, or to perceive spiritual influences attached to objects or locations, He does so with purpose. Revelation brings responsibility. At times, the response may be intercession; at other times, it may require direct spiritual warfare. Sometimes what is revealed is meant to be shared with the right leaders; other times, it calls for silent prayer and humble obedience. Scripture reminds us that *"from everyone who has been given much, much will be required"* and *"freely you have received, freely give"* (Luke 12:48; Matthew 10:8). If the Lord has entrusted you with this kind of discernment, let humility, not pride, be your covering.

Setting the Land and Buildings Free

We were not redeemed to remain helpless victims of evil. Just as individuals can be forgiven, cleansed, and healed through repentance, so land, buildings, and homes can also be cleansed and restored in the same way. Inner healing is a process of sanctification—the application of the cross, the blood, and the resurrection life of Jesus to areas of history that have not yet been redeemed. For redemption to occur, the root cause or "open door" that allowed demonic access must be identified and closed. This often includes repentance and renunciation related to the actions of previous occupants or owners. Inner healing always addresses the cause in order to dismantle the stronghold, while deliverance removes what has taken residence there.

Whether the issue involves a person, an animal, a place, or an object, inner healing and deliverance must work together. If we attempt to heal history without removing demonic influence, progress is often blocked and healing remains incomplete. Conversely, if demons are expelled without healing what allowed access in the first place, the unhealed "house" can invite them back and once again provide a place to dwell.

The process of freeing land, buildings, and organizations from specific demonic control closely parallels the way a person is set free. In personal deliverance, confession and repentance form the foundation for healing and freedom where sin has given the enemy access. When a person has been sinned against and becomes vulnerable—often through trauma—forgiveness becomes a vital part of the healing process. At its core, deliverance seeks to identify how the enemy gained legal ground in a person's life.

In the same way, when addressing land, buildings, or organizations, we must ask similar questions: What occurred in the past that gave the enemy rights or authority? The issue is not possession of a person, but the granting of influence or control over a place, structure, or system. Identifying and addressing those roots allows true cleansing, restoration, and lasting freedom to take place.

When ministering to land or buildings, legal rights are critically important. Whom holds legal ownership of the property matters, because legal authority establishes the basis for exercising spiritual authority. If you are a tenant, your authority is limited to binding any demonic influence so it does not affect you or your activities within the building. However, if you are the legal owner and desire to cleanse the property, you carry the spiritual authority to do so by virtue of your legal ownership.

The Cleansing Process:

1.　　　Establish who has the legal authority over the land or buildings to be cleansed. The legal authority should be involved in the cleansing process as they have spiritual authority.

2.　　　There are two aspects of the process, the first being what originally happened to the land and buildings before the present owner acquired the property? And the second, what has happened to the property during the present term of ownership?

3.　　　Discover what ungodliness is tied to what has happened in this place during previous ownership – occult activities, violence, sexual violation, criminal activities, financial mismanagement. All of these circumstances give Satan hold of the spiritual title to the property.

4.　　　Confess all that you know has happened on the property. Your confession is an agreement about what God thinks about these things. As a legal owner, declare that you forgive everyone involved. Be specific and release them into the freedom of your forgiveness. Then declare into the heavenly realms that you now have legal and spiritual authority and that any powers of darkness operating over the property no longer have any rights to stay. Exercise your Kingdom authority to set the land and buildings free.

5.   Turn your attention to everything you know has happened during the present ownership and deal with it in a similar way. Where those in authority hold personal responsibility for these matters, it calls for confession, repentance, and a commitment to put things right.

6.   After implementing the above steps, we have usually go around the perimeter of the land, anointing any fence posts with oil, declaring the authority of Jesus over the land and telling the powers of darkness that they have to leave. Do the same for each building, praying and praising each room of the building, not forgetting to pray in the basements, attics and the land under the building.

7.   Sometimes this can be a process and we have to stay open to the voice of the Holy Spirit. Step by step you should sense the spiritual atmosphere changing for the good as each place is cleansed, and see His authority increasingly lifted up over and in the property.

Defiled Homes

Many so-called "haunted houses" appear to be occupied by what seems to be former residents or families who once lived there. This often occurs in places where tragedy has taken place—especially sudden, violent deaths or suicides—situations in which demonic activity has operated with unusual intensity. In such cases, these manifestations are not the departed themselves but familiar spirits masquerading as them. Most Christians hold that when a person dies, they immediately enter judgment, and God determines their eternal destination (Luke 16:26).

A home is not defiled only by its history or by the actions of previous occupants. At times, it is the objects brought into the home that introduce defilement. Scripture warns against bringing abominable or cursed items into our dwellings. Deuteronomy 7:26 states, *"Do not bring a detestable thing into your house or you, like it, will be set apart for destruction. Regard it as vile and utterly detest it, for it is set apart for destruction."* We have often found that people struggle to walk in freedom because they possess objects that are cursed or inhabited by demonic influence. These items can exert significant spiritual control, and they are frequently pieces of jewelry, antiques or objects of high personal or monetary value.

Once we understand how curses can affect a person through the agency of unclean spirits, it becomes easier to see how those same spirits can attach themselves to objects and places. Those who live in or interact with such environments may then come under the influence of the spirits connected to them.

As a real estate broker and owner/general contractor of a flood restoration company, I often see that one of the most common causes of flooding in a home is a failed wax ring beneath a toilet—something that is invisible at the time of purchase. For this reason, when I hand over the keys to a previously occupied home, I recommend that all toilets be removed and the wax rings be replaced, because the activity of the former occupants is unknown. The same principle applies spiritually. Even though you now hold legal title and authority, the past actions of previous owners may have left doors open. Therefore, the land and the home should be cleansed and dedicated to God.

If sin—especially repeated sin—was practiced in the home or on the land, demonic access points may remain open until they are intentionally closed. Even under new ownership, the enemy will attempt to exploit these openings to harass or oppress you and your family. Removing such influence and restoring peace to the home requires intentional cleansing and, when necessary, deliverance.

Here are some symptoms of spiritual pollution in your home:
Continual bad dreams and nightmares, Insomnia (inability to sleep peacefully); Behavioral and relational problems among adults or children (continual fighting or misunderstanding); Lack of peace, disturbed/tormented children; Unexplained and ongoing illnesses (such as chronic headache, nausea or

fatigue); Heightened bondages (increased mental or physical perversion); Ghosts or demonic apparitions (especially when children are visited frequently); Poltergeist (the movement of physical objects by demons), Foul unexplainable odors and Atmospheric heaviness (which makes it hard to breath); and Continual financial difficulties.

Defiled Objects

In 2 Chronicles 29, Hezekiah Purified the Temple. He called the priests and Levites to consecrate themselves and the Temple of the Lord by removing all defilement from the Temple of the Lord. King Hezekiah attributed the defilement to their parents who were unfaithful as they did evil in the eyes of the Lord and turned their backs on him (2 Chronicles 29:5-6). The priests consecrated themselves and removed all the defiled things from the Temple, cleansing the utensils, the altar and the table (2 Chronicles 29:16).

Before cleansing a home, we first walk through every room and ask the Holy Spirit for guidance to identify any unclean or defiling objects. Often, those affected by a curse have unknowingly come into possession of something that is cursed or connected to a cursed place. Or they may be holding onto old items or gifts from a former relationship, solidifying a soul tie. Without understanding how this works spiritually, they may have no framework for recognizing why they are suffering or experiencing oppression.

On one occasion, a woman came to the altar for deliverance, yet she was not receiving freedom despite prayer from several people. As I walked by, the Holy Spirit drew my attention to the necklace she was wearing. I recognized it as a dreamcatcher. Dreamcatchers are rooted in witchcraft and, in practice, function in direct opposition to their claimed purpose. By owning or displaying one, a person unintentionally signals belief in its supernatural power to filter dreams or ward off evil. In reality, such items act as beacons to demonic spirits seeking influence, a host, or territory.

Much like a rabbit's foot or horseshoe that are believed to bring luck, these objects create what Scripture would describe as fertile soil for occult influence. They function as talismans or amulets, similar to the idols and pagan icons the Bible warns against—objects that point to a source of spiritual power in opposition to Jesus Christ. When worn, they bring defilement to the person, and when brought into a home, they defile the environment as well.

After explaining to the woman the spiritual significance of the necklace, I asked her whether she still wanted to keep it. I always ask this question, because when the removal or destruction of such an object is proposed, demonic resistance often manifests. Spirits may react with fear, produce seemingly rational arguments for keeping the object, or even attempt to prevent its removal through sudden strength or disruption.

Once the woman understood that this necklace had been one of the enemy's tools to influence and bind her, she immediately tore it from her neck and threw it down at the altar. After a simple prayer, she was completely set free. Later, the necklace was destroyed.

There is often a progression when it comes to detestable or defiling objects. Many people dismiss the spiritual impact of keeping an old love letter connected to a soul tie, hanging a dreamcatcher over a baby's crib, purchasing secondhand jewelry that carries the imprint of a previous owner, or bringing home statues, masks, or artifacts from third-world countries that were crafted or used in occult practices. Just as every seed is designed to produce a harvest, every foothold seeks to grow into a stronghold within a home.

Cursed jewelry is frequently inherited, which is why one of the first questions we ask when someone begins experiencing sudden or unusual problems is, "Have you inherited or acquired any objects that may link to an occult or troubled history?" The same question applies to secondhand jewelry. Used engagement rings, for example, can carry a curse into a marriage when they were previously associated with broken engagements, divorce, or unresolved trauma. For this reason, we strongly caution against purchasing secondhand jewelry, as the spiritual history attached to it is often unknown.

Items from former relationships—such as clothing, gifts, photographs, or love letters—can also give the enemy influence through lingering sexual or emotional soul ties. Likewise, keeping urns containing the remains of deceased loved ones or animals can bind individuals through unhealthy psychological attachments. In some cases, we have also discovered that people unknowingly keep objects that were used in witchcraft, unaware of the influence those items continue to exert in their lives.

Used items given to our children can carry many of the same concerns as secondhand jewelry. We must be discerning about toys, blankets, or clothing passed on to our children, as these items may come from environments influenced by witchcraft or spoken curses. An unhealthy or unnatural attachment to a toy or blanket can become a point of bondage, not only in childhood but later in life as well.

In general, only objects that have been directly used in occult practices need to be physically destroyed. Deuteronomy 7:25 instructs us to destroy occult objects by fire. However, if there is any unhealthy attachment to a gift or possession, we recommend that it be prayed over, consecrated to the Lord with anointing oil, and that any ungodly soul ties associated with it be broken.

Acts 19 provides a clear example of spiritual housecleaning. As the gospel spread throughout Ephesus, *"many who believed came confessing and declaring their practices. And many of those who practiced magic brought their books together and burned them in the sight of all."* The believers in Ephesus destroyed occult items valued at approximately four million dollars, demonstrating their commitment to freedom and holiness.

Spiritual Housecleaning

In 2 Chronicles 29, after the priests and Levites under King Hezekiah consecrated themselves and removed every defilement from the temple of the Lord, they then began the consecration of the Temple itself—a process that took eight days (2 Chronicles 29:17).

As stated earlier, we approach a home in the same way we would a person when ministering deliverance and inner healing. First, we seek to understand the cause that allowed evil influences to remain. We create an atmosphere of forgiveness to close any open doors, and then we bind and break every authority that has empowered those influences to dwell in the home. Because it is a house, lay hands on the doorframes and plead the blood of Jesus. This act is symbolic of Exodus 12:22, when Israel applied the blood to the doorposts with hyssop. Pleading the blood of Jesus addresses sin issues and establishes redemption.

Based on this pattern, here are the steps for purification:

1. Anoint the front doorframe with anointing oil and invite the Holy Spirit into the home. Your peace must be received (see Matthew 10:13). All it takes is one believer in the home to make the whole home and family holy (1 Corinthians 7:14).

2. Walk through the home and sprinkle every room with Holy Water. When we walk through the home, we will pray as led and will sprinkle every room with Holy Water that represents the washing of the word and ask the Holy Spirit to sanctify it (Acts 5:26, John 13:5-10).

   a. If, when we go through the home, we see something manifest, we are to bind it and cast it into the hands of Jesus. It is unscriptural to pronounce judgment. If the Lord has not yet cast the fallen angels into the Lake of Fire, but holds them captive till the day of Judgment, then it is our responsibility to cast out demons and turn them over to Jesus and allow Him to do as He wills.

3. Remove and destroy (not give away) items related to the occult, heathen worship, past sin and anything else the Holy Spirit convicts you of. You are responsible for what God shows you to do, and as you do it, you are sanctified (James 4:17).

   a. Deuteronomy 7:25 states, *"The images of their gods you are to burn in the fire. Do not covet the silver and gold on them, and do not take it for yourselves, or **you will be ensnared by it**, for it is detestable to the LORD your God."*

4. Repent for the sins and behaviors of both you and your family members (see 1 John 1:7-10).

5. Repent on behalf of past owners for any defilement in the land or house. God has given us dominion over the earth. *"May the Lord who created the heavens and the earth*

give you His blessing. The Lord has kept the heavens for himself, but he has given the earth to us humans" (Psalms 115:15-16).

6.　　Renounce aloud any demonic contract that you have made willingly or unwillingly and break any unholy covenants with past sin. (Detail your renouncing. For example, you may want to pray, "I sever any and all unholy soul ties bound to me while in the ungodly relationship with [insert the name of the person]. I break them now by the blood of Jesus.)

7.　　Command the demons, in the name of Jesus, to leave you, your family and your home. Ask the Lord to cleanse you, your possessions and your home.

　　a.　　**Sample prayer for the homeowners:** *Lord, as the homeowners of this house, we want to thank You for the gift you have given us. We thank you for the protection of our home and children. Your Word states in 1 John 4:4, "You are of God, little children, and have overcome them, because He who is in you Is greater than he who is in the world." It is from this authority of You living in us that we pray. We say in agreement that all demonic spirits inhabiting this home must go now, in Jesus' name. All spirits of death, leave now. All perversion and activities of sexual abuse, we command you to leave our property. [Insert the spirits that are in operation in the home], you will no longer harass our family. You have been given your eviction notice. Your assignment here is canceled. We proclaim that you will not return to this home or land.*

8.　　Communion rededicates the home to the Lord. It makes a statement to all the powers of darkness that it is because of the death and resurrection of the Lord Jesus Christ that Christians need not fear the activities of Satan and can live in freedom from ongoing influence of his demons in the house (see Isaiah 53:5, Jude 1:6).

　　a.　　2 Chronicles 29:21-24, *"Hezekiah rededicated the Temple and Israel to the Lord by way of covenant. Israel got together in the sanctuary and offered a sacrifice of bulls, rams, lambs, goats and their blood as the sin offering for atonement."*

　　b.　　Hebrews 10:8-14 says, *"First he said, 'Sacrifices and offerings, burnt offerings and sin offerings you did not desire, nor were you pleased with them'—though they were offered in accordance with the law. Then he said, 'Here I am, I have come to do your will.' He sets aside the first to establish the second. And by that will, we have been made holy through the sacrifice of the body of Jesus Christ once for all. Day after day every priest stands and performs his religious duties; again and again he offers the same sacrifices, which can never take away sins. But when this priest had offered for all time one sacrifice for sins, he sat down at the right hand of God, and since that time he waits for his enemies to be made his footstool. For by one sacrifice he has made perfect forever those who are being made holy."* Communion is a prophetic act that will bring forth a spiritual breakthrough.

9.　　Dedicate the home to the Lord.

　　a.　　**Sample Prayer:** *Lord, we desire holiness as You are holy. We bring our home before You, dedicating it to You and Your purposes. May Your peace, love and joy fill our dwelling. Where there has been demonic activity, we welcome the activity of Your angels in the walls of this house and the boundaries of this property. We proclaim, "As for me and our house, we will serve the Lord."*

10.　　Deslime before you Leave.

Periodic Cleansing or Desliming from Warfare and Defilement

Sometimes places need to be cleansed not because of long-term habitation, but because of recent ministry and spiritual warfare. I once spoke with Pastor Kumara in Liberia, Africa, who specializes in deliverance. He emphasized the importance of "desliming" both himself *and* his home after ministry. On one occasion, he shared that a demon he had cast out of a person followed him home and attempted to attach itself to one of his children. He had to confront it again, casting it off his child and out of his home in order to restore peace and freedom.

After ministering to those who are demonized, it is important to take time to remove any spiritual residue from the encounter. Ask the Lord to wash you thoroughly, to cancel every assignment of hell, and to release the assignments of heaven over you and your team. Pray for purity of mind, guarded emotions, protection over your body, and grace to bless those who may oppose or curse you.

Lord Jesus, I plead the blood of Jesus over my life and over the lives of my family. I ask that you cleanse me with your blood and I hereby cancel any assignment of hell or its agents, and release the assignments of heaven over our lives. Lord Jesus, bless me and keep me by keeping my mind pure, help me to guard my emotions against anything that would come against my knowledge of you, protect my body from sickness and disease and I bless those who would curse me, in Jesus' name.

We need to pray regularly over ourselves, our homes, our churches, and our places of employment. Prayer keeps us sanctified and proactive. When we stay on the offense, the enemy is pushed back and loses ground.

When I was four years old, I slept on the top bunk while my older brother slept below me. On many nights, a demon would appear on the ceiling above my bed, making grotesque faces at me. One night it would not leave. I climbed down from my bed and looked out the window, only to see another grotesque figure standing on the carport roof, staring in at me through the window. I told my mother what I had seen, but she assumed I had just woken from a bad dream and told me to go back to bed—yet I was fully awake.

Years later, when both of my sons turned four, they experienced strikingly similar episodes. When Eli was four, he told me that a figure appeared on the ceiling of his bedroom. I was stunned, because it was the same type of manifestation I had experienced at that age. When Eli saw it again, Kristen went into his room, took authority over the spirit, bound it, and released it to Jesus. It never returned.

When Aden turned four, he began having night-terrors that would not stop. I felt led by the Lord to enter into a fast that lasted two weeks. At the end of that time, I had a dream in which the Lord showed me Aden being protected by three blue spiders under his bed. I asked the Lord what the spiders represented, and He explained that they were neither good nor evil—but hungry. He showed me that the access point for the demonic activity was under Aden's bed, and that the spiders had built webs there and set up camp. The following morning, we realized Aden had slept through the entire night without a single night-terror. The Lord told me the spiders would remain until all the "food" — the demonic presence — had been consumed.

Visitations at Night

After I was saved, I experienced nightly visitations from what missionaries in Africa referred to as a "black wraith." Night after night, I was attacked by demonic forces and instantly paralyzed—unable to move, unable even to open my mouth to say the name of Jesus. In those moments, I would cry out internally to Him until I gradually regained control of my mouth and could command the demons to leave me and my room. These experiences have often caused me to wonder whether similar spiritual assaults could be connected to phenomena such as sudden infant death syndrome (also known as SIDS).

At times, people who are involved in sexual sin can attract incubus or succubus spirits. In such cases, repentance is necessary, and sexual soul ties must be broken. In other instances, these attacks occur during seasons of spiritual breakthrough, when the enemy uses moments of rest or vulnerability to torment a person. When this happens, it is important to seek the Lord concerning the root cause.

In my own life, these visitations continued nightly for two years. I grew deeply frustrated, having sought prayer from many leaders and ministries—including ministers promoting Lester Sumrall's ministry—yet the attacks did not stop. At the end of those two years, the Lord spoke clearly to me and said, "Authority is not recognized unless it is challenged." Demons had encountered as a child, the manifestations I saw during the day, and the nightly visitations were all preparation for the deliverance ministry He was calling me into.

Avoiding Accidents

I have heard people describe frightening experiences—one person said they were pushed down a staircase by an unseen force, while another shared that when she jumped into a lake, something seemed to pull her feet down, preventing her from reaching the surface. Accounts like these reinforce my conviction that we should regularly pray for our homes and workplaces to be cleansed of any defiling or attacking spirits.

Here is another simple prayer:

Lord Jesus, if any spirits have attached themselves to us or our home today, we ask that You send Your angels to remove them. Cleanse us and our home as the only Spirit allowed is the Holy Spirit. Thank You, Lord.

Chapter 10 — Prayers

Identity always determines your impact because it either limits or enables your access to the Kingdom of God by the Spirit of God. Many Christians have a "high value" for the Word of God and can memorize scriptures but pressure will determine if it is a "core value". Core values are what a person actually believes as it controls the lens they see everything through. Faith will take a "high value" and transform it into a "core value". What you see is not as important as how you see it. Prayer allows you to see life through a new lens. This is why Luke 8:18 says, *"take care of how you hear"* as faith comes by hearing. Job 22:28 says, *"You will also decide and decree a thing, and it will be established for you; And the light [of God's favor] will shine upon your ways."*

This chapter will provide you with many different prayers that are useful when performing inner healing or deliverance sessions. Allow them to be used as a guide for you to build upon as you heal others with your prayers.

Identity Statement for Ministering Deliverance – For Prayer Counselor:
"I am a child of the King; I am a co-heir with Jesus. All Jesus bought and paid for is my inheritance. I am united with Jesus; I have been crucified with Christ. I died with Him, I was buried with Him, I was raised with Him, I am seated with Him in the heavenlies far above all rule, all power, all authority, and above every name that is named, not only in this age, but also in the one to come. Therefore, I carry the authority Christ. I have authority over sickness, over sin, over demons, and over the world. I am the salt of the earth; I am the light of the world. I will displace the darkness; I have the full armor of God. I put on the breastplate of righteousness, the belt of truth, the helmet of salvation, the sandals of peace, I take up the shield of faith and the sword of the Spirit, for the weapons of my warfare are not fleshly. They are divinely powerful to tear down the strongholds of darkness. I can do all things through Christ, because greater is He who is in me than he who is in the world."

Prayers for Prayee or Person Receiving Deliverance and/or Inner Healing to State Aloud:

- **Identity and Doctrinal Affirmation:**

"There is only one true and living God, who exists as the Father, Son, and Holy Spirit. Jesus is the Christ and the only way to the Father. Jesus destroyed the works of the devil. He disarmed the rulers and authorities, having triumphed over them through His shed blood on the cross. Jesus now has all authority in heaven and on earth. Jesus has authority over sin, He has authority over sickness, He has authority over death, He has authority over the world, He has authority over the devil. He has redeemed me from hell and has given me a new destiny. I am saved by grace through faith and not of my own works. Jesus delivered me from the domain of darkness and transferred me to His kingdom. I have been forgiven of all my sin. I am now ONE with Jesus. I died with Christ, I was buried with Christ, I rose with Christ. I am seated with Jesus in the heavenlies. Because I am one with Jesus, I am righteous, I am holy, I am a saint and I will live above sin. Because I am prone to do righteousness, I am not prone toward sin any more. I am a new creature, the old is gone, the new has come. Because of my oneness of Jesus, I have authority over sin, over the world, and over the devil. I can resist the devil and he will flee from me. God has given me spiritual weapons and spiritual armor. I can live a victorious life. I can do all things through Christ. I will overcome in this world, because greater is He who is in me than he who is in the world."

- **Binding and Loosening:** Bind Evil Spirits and Loose the Person (There blood of Jesus is effective as there has to be a covenant to bind the demon to). "Father, I come to you in the name of Jesus, and plead the blood of Jesus over _____. Your word says (Name the scripture the deals with the wound) and I declare your word over their life knowing it will hit its mark and prosper in the area I send it. Spirit of _____ (name of evil Spirit), I bind you under the blood of Jesus Christ and declare you are powerless to harm or harass _____ (prayee name) or his/her family." (Praise and pause until you feel the spirit leave). "Father, in the name of Jesus, I here by release _____ (prayee name) from the powers of darkness and into the freedom of your Kingdom and the freedom and glory of the children of God." (You can go further to loose love in replace of hate, etc.)

- **Breaking Generational Curses:** *(by Rodney Hogue)* "Heavenly Father, according to my covenant with you, I ask You to open the books of my past, of every covenant made by my forefathers that they entered into on my behalf that is giving protection to the demonic around me. Look at these, Heavenly Father, and see if any of these are not absolutely just and righteous. Then, annul them and release the affliction of the demonic on me."

- **Specific Generational Declaration:** Exodus 20:5 and Numbers 14:18 states that generational curses go to the third and fourth generations so you can start with the fourth generation and work your way back to you.

"In the name of Jesus, we declare the blood of Jesus to stand between me and the _____ generation as a wall of separation. I cancel every assignment of darkness and remove every right of the demonic to afflict me because of the sin of that generation. I break the legal rights of all generational spirits operating behind the curse and I break every oath, vow and pact made with the devil by my ancestors in the name of Jesus. Jesus bore the curse on my behalf, therefore no undeserved curse can find rest in my life. I call onto me my righteous inheritance and declare that every curse spoken against my me or my ancestors be turned into the blessings in Jesus name."

- **Breaking the Curse of Words:** "Father, I come to you, in the name of Jesus, and I break every curse of words against me. I take every word captive that has been spoken over me or that I spoke over myself. I break the power of those curses as I am no landing path for a curse. I cancel every assignment of darkness and I cast them to the ground to be without effect. I call blessings to fall on me in its place. I take back every curse that I have spoken against another. I cast those words down to the ground to be without effect. I return a blessing on those whom I have cursed. Jesus took my curse so I can live in blessing."

- **Breaking the Curse of Words Due to Being Labeled Badly:** "Father, I come to you, in the name of Jesus. I was called _____. Forgive me for receiving it and believing the lie. I renounce you and take back the authority I gave over to you. I bind you, in the name of Jesus, and I command every negative influence to leave my life, never to trouble me again. I plead the blood of Jesus over my heart and life to stand as a wall of separation between us. Holy Spirit, come into my heart and my life and I ask that you fill every place in my heart the enemy once influenced and occupied." **Affirmation:** "I am a child of the King adopted into the family of God. I am known by God as Son/Daughter; I am a co-heir with Jesus. All Jesus bought and paid for is my inheritance. I am loved. I am forgiven. I am cleaned by the blood of Jesus." **Stay in this place and listen for any words the Holy Spirit may say to you about your identity.**

- **Breaking Physical Soul Ties:** "In the authority of Jesus, I plead the blood of Jesus to stand between me and _____ to separate the 'one flesh' union. I send back to _____ everything that I have taken from him/her in the one flesh union and I call back to me everything that I gave to him/her in that union. I declare the blood of Jesus to be a wall of separation between us. Thank You Jesus for restoring my soul."

- **Breaking Psychological Soul Tie:** or Loss of a Loved one with Continued Mourning. "Lord Jesus, I thank you that you carried my grief and my sorrows so I would not have to. Forgive me for believing the lies and allowing the enemy to torment me and gain ground in my heart through my loss. I lift _____ up to you and release him/her into your hands. Your word is the sword of the Spirit with the power to divide all things that oppose Your knowledge and Your will for my life. In the name of Jesus, I sever every demonic entanglement and attachment to any and all wrongful emotional, mental, spiritual and physical ties with _____. I plead the blood of Jesus to stand as a wall of separation between us. Holy Spirit, I receive your oil of joy instead of mourning and a garment of praise instead of a spirit of despair. Come into my heart and my life and fill me in every place the enemy once influenced and occupied, in the mighty name of Jesus."

- **Forgiveness:** "In the name of Jesus, I choose to forgive as I have been forgiven. I now choose to forgive _____. I release any right I have retained to bring revenge. I release them from my hands and place them into Your hands, Jesus, my Just Judge. I break every curse I have sent to them and call forth a blessing to them instead. Thank you for the grace to forgive and the power to live in freedom."

- **Forgiving God:** (associated with Pride) "Father, I come to you, in the name of Jesus, and I thank you for being faithful in your love towards me even when I was faithless. Forgive me for mistakenly believing the lies for what the enemy, or others under his direction, have done to me. You said you will never leave me nor forsake me and I know this is the truth. I have never been left alone and have never been forsaken. Thank you that these barriers I placed between us are now removed. I thank you for your mercy and grace and ask that you help me to love you more and with that love, walk in a deeper more intimate relationship with you, in Jesus' name."

- **Post-Prayer for Prayer Counselor:** "Lord Jesus, I plead the blood of Jesus over my life and over the lives of my family. I ask that you cleanse me with your blood and I hereby cancel any assignment of hell, and release the assignments of heaven over our lives. Lord Jesus, bless me and keep me by keeping my mind pure, help me to guard my emotions against anything that would come against my knowledge of you, protect my body from sickness and disease and I bless those who would curse me, in Jesus' name."

- **Removing Bonds of Fear:** "Father, in the name of Jesus, I renounce fear and choose to live in your perfect love that casts out fear. I cast off the yoke of domination and I choose to forgive _____ for believing the lies that I was unloved. I break the power of their words over me. I break the victim spirit off of me. I rebuke the fear of man and the rejection I have lived under. I cancel my bond to them. I take back my true identity as a son/daughter of God as His beloved. The love of God has not only sustained me but given me hope for the future He has created for me. Lord Jesus, I thank you for your grace that has enabled me to not only be free but to live, to laugh and to love again, in Jesus' name."

- **Renouncing Habitual Sin:** "Lord Jesus, I renounce the use of my body as an instrument of unrighteousness. I acknowledge that I have given in to fleshly lusts that wage war against my soul. I confess that I have willfully chose to rebel against You and Your word which states that we are to live life by the spirit and not to fulfill the desires of the flesh. Therefore, I confess to you my sinful habit of _____. Forgive me for violating my trust in you and heal every heart-wound that enabled me to open the doors of temptation, leading me away from you. Satan, in the name of Jesus, I bind you, according the Matthew 18:18, which gives me the authority to bind and loose on earth as it is in heaven. I hereby cancel every assignment, every entanglement and every attachment that opened the door of temptation and held me captive to it. I plead the blood of Jesus over it as a wall of separation between us. Lord Jesus, thank you for forgiving me and setting me free. By the blood of Jesus, I receive the cleansing of my mind and body. I declare that sin will not be my master, for in Christ I am now prone to righteousness. I receive the grace to obey You and resist temptation. Thank you that you love me unconditionally. I love you, Lord."

- **Renouncing the Involvement in Occult or Cult Practices:** "Father, in the name of Jesus, I renounce any involvement in _____ (name the occult or cultic practice). I renounce _____ (list the teaching/practice involved in). In the name of Jesus and by the blood of Jesus, I bind you and command you to leave my life. Father, forgive me for worshipping other Gods. I declare that Jesus is the way, the truth and the life. No one comes to the Father but through Jesus. I declare that Jesus is the Lord of my life and will worship Him and Him alone. Holy Spirit, fill me in every place the enemy once influenced and occupied, in Jesus' name."

- **Renouncing Sexual Perversion:** (by Rodney Hogue, *Liberated)* "Father, in the name of Jesus, I break all attachments to lust, perversion, fantasy, and sexual immorality. I repent for viewing pornography for sexual stimulation, satisfaction, comfort, and escape. I repent for any addiction of reading or viewing that captures my emotions in fantasy. I confess that I have committed adultery in my heart. I confess every act of sexual perversion with my body. I humbly ask for your forgiveness. By the blood of Jesus, cleanse me from the shame, humiliation, and filthiness that have clung to me from my defilement. In the name of Jesus, I bind the enemy and cancel and cleanse my mind of wrongful images and wash my heart, returning it to purity. I commit myself to see others as God's valuable creation and will give them the honor that God does. I commit my mind, imagination, and emotions to You, my Lord. I choose to dwell on things that are true, noble, right and pure, in Jesus' name."

- **Substance Abuse Prayer:** (by Rodney Hogue, *Liberated*) "I confess that I have misused _____ (alcohol, tobacco, food, drugs) for the purpose of _____ (pleasure, to escape reality, or to cope with difficult situations). I repent for ensnaring myself and becoming a slave to substances and allowing evil powers to rule over me. I renounce any demonic connection or influence in my life through my misuse of _____. Forgive me for abusing my body and quenching the Holy Spirit. I commit myself to no longer yield to _____, but to yield to the Holy Spirit. I admit to my responsibility for damaging my relationships. I bind the authority I gave over to the enemy and take back dominion over my life that I gave over to demonic influence. Father, in the name of Jesus, fill me with your spirit, to not only occupy the places the enemy once occupied and influenced, but heal those I have hurt to strengthen them, restore them and bless them, in Jesus' name."

- **The Spirit of Religion**: *"*In the name of Jesus, I renounce every spirit of religion and every work of darkness connected with it. I repent for allowing myself to be led by any spirit other than the Holy Spirit. I renounce all forms of legalism, traditions of man, and participation in dead works. I repent of my hypocrisy, pride, and arrogance. I repent of relying on my own works and self-righteousness to find favor in the sight of God and man. I repent of relying on my own intellect rather than your Holy Spirit and for inappropriately using scripture as a weapon to bring harm to other saints. Forgive me for my false judgements, criticism, gossip, jealously, covetousness, anger, and hardness of heart. Forgive me for slandering and persecuting those who are moving in the Holy Spirit and for attributing the works of the Holy Spirit to the devil. I renounce any belief that portrays You, Lord, as distant and judgmental and I receive the fullness of Your love, compassion, mercy, and grace. I choose to embrace all of the aspects of Your true character and to know you intimately."

Chapter 11 — Our Inner Healing Packet

Over the course of our ministry, we have had the opportunity to network with several other ministries in order to build, what we believe to be, a well-rounded packet for people to fill out prior to an inner healing session with our prayer counselors. Using guided prayers (such as the ones from chapters 10 and 12), you are able to walk them through the common causes of wounds. Below, is our full packet that we have compiled for your use:

INNER HEALING PACKET

Deliverance comes through the guidance of the Holy Spirit and does not follow a specific method or formula. Healing does not occur without revelation. Many desire relief from symptoms without allowing God to reveal the root cause. The effectiveness of healing depends on a heart that is honest, open, and willing to submit.

There is no salvation or deliverance apart from Christ. For deliverance to be effective, the presence of Christ in a person's life is essential. Those in need of deliverance have previously been under spiritual bondage and the influence of the devil. As John 8:34 states, *"Everyone who sins is a slave to sin."* Freedom from the devil's control comes only through submitting every area of life to the authority and Lordship of Jesus Christ. John 8:36 affirms, *"So if the Son sets you free, you will be free indeed."*

We acknowledge that all of us carry baggage from past experiences and backgrounds that can hinder spiritual growth and limit our ability to fully receive God's love for ourselves and for others. This is a safe space to be healed and released from past wounds. God honors free will, and authority cannot be broken where it has not first been surrendered. Likewise, demonic influence cannot be removed unless that place is first yielded to Christ. It is not possible to minister deliverance to someone who has not expressed a genuine desire to submit every area of their life to the Lordship of Jesus. When God is given authority, He releases His power in every area of life.

Willful disobedience represents areas that have **not** been surrendered to Christ. This may include lifestyles involving substance abuse, sexual activity outside of marriage, or unwillingness to remain rooted in a church community. Scripture teaches that when two people become one flesh, there can be both physical and spiritual consequences. These may include soul ties, vows, or spiritual entanglements. If one individual has been involved in practices such as witchcraft, sorcery, or psychic activity, those spiritual influences may gain access to the other person through that union.

If there are areas of your life that you are unwilling to surrender to the Lordship of Jesus Christ, then deliverance is **not appropriate for you at this time**. Those who desire freedom but are unwilling to abandon former practices cannot receive deliverance and expect lasting freedom. Therefore, it is not appropriate to minister deliverance to individuals who express a desire to be free yet neither accept Christ nor turn away from practices that violate God's will for their lives.

Please, prayerfully, consider your response to each section, asking the Holy Spirit to bring understanding and clarity. All information shared is kept confidential. Each person is encouraged to "pray first" and seek the Lord regarding whether He is leading them to participate. If, to the best of your ability, you sense that God is leading you to come, then trust that He desires to extend His grace to bring freedom—regardless of personal preferences concerning methods or ministry approaches. Deliverance begins, as all blessings from God do, with a decision. Choose freedom, and having made that decision, do not allow anything or anyone to hinder you from receiving it. Deliverance and inner healing, by the power of the Holy Spirit, have brought profound transformation in many lives. Many describe the experience as life-changing, so come with expectation and openness to new beginnings.

For deliverance to be successful and lasting, it is essential that these instructions are followed. Come determined to be free, willing to be transparent, teachable, humble, and ready to release, repent, and forgive. If you are unwilling to follow the guidelines provided, do not expect ministry or deliverance. Do not come out of curiosity or for entertainment; deliverance is a serious and sacred step in the life of a believer. This is the work of God, and everything is done unto the Lord.

In some cases, complete and lasting deliverance may require more than one session. This depends on the leading of the Holy Spirit and your willingness to cooperate fully with His work. Each person's journey is unique, and as stated earlier, what has worked for one individual may not be the same for another.

I, _____, agree to submit every area of my life to the Lordship of Jesus, foregoing any willful involvement of disobedient lifestyle choices. I will abide by the guidelines that are given to me not only when I am preparing for and receiving ministry, but after I have received my deliverance as well. I am ready to receive deliverance and fully commit myself to my healing process.

Signature: _____ Date: _____

PRE-DELIVERANCE INSTRUCTIONS

1. Fasting is required the day prior to the session and throughout the entire workshop unless prior approval for medical reasons have been given:
   a. No solid foods, only liquids such as juice, tea, milk, protein shake, water, etc. Beverages will be provided upon request.
   b. When you arrive, you will be asked if you have eaten that day. If you have, you will be asked to reschedule for the next available time slot.
2. Eat a significant amount of protein within few days prior to the workshop to strengthen your immune system and provide energy.
3. Get plenty of rest!
4. Wear comfortable clothes – sweat suits, etc. Women: no low-cut tops, tight clothing, dresses, skirts or jewelry.
5. Be on time.
6. Bring your Bible.
7. Bring a pen and paper for any personal notes you may wish to take.
8. Plan on four hours for your session. The session is in depth and spiritually rewarding.

IMMEDIATE CHANGES TO EXPECT AFTER THE SEMINAR

There are nine areas of immediate and noticeable changes that result from the Inner Healing and Deliverance Seminar:

1. Release in praise and worship of God (ability to enter His presence)
2. Greater discernment of the enemy and kingdom of darkness
3. Less "voices," noise and chattering in the mind
4. Easier time reading and richer studying of God's Word (Bible)
5. Increase in the anointing to minister
6. Immense peace
7. Greater love, compassion, and understanding towards others
8. Greater understanding and ability to learn about spiritual warfare and deliverance
9. Closer relationship and walk with Jesus, and an awakening in your spirit.

INNER HEALING/SPIRITUAL WARFARE PARTICIPANT CHECKLIST

Please **initial** the list below to ensure you are prepared to attend the Inner Healing Session with _____ (name of church), and that you have agreed to participate in these activities. **Hand in prior to arrival of your scheduled session day, (Date):** _____

_____ 1. I have read the required books "*Forgiveness*" and "*Liberated*" by Rodney Hogue, and any others assigned to me (optional): _____

_____ 2. I have circled/listed those items pertaining to me on the following forms I have received: **Ancestral (family background), Biblical Curse Sheet, Broken Vows and Soul Ties, Detestable Objects, Inner Healing Life Cycles and Snares/Open Doors.**

_____ 3. I have read the included sheets on **Forgiveness** and **Communion.**

_____ 4. I agree to a liquid fast for participation. (Subject to medical condition, that I have discussed with ministry staff ahead of time).

_____ 5. I agree to dress comfortably, but appropriately: (women are strongly encouraged to wear pants, nothing short, tight or low cut. Jeans, leggings, sweats suits, etc. are appropriate).

_____ 6. I have rested and prepared myself physically (healthy eating / sleeping) and spiritually (prayer) for ministry.

_____ 7. I have signed and agree to all terms in the **Inner Healing Agreement Form** (first page).

I hereby affirm that I have done all with the help of the Holy Spirit to prepare myself to receive ministry during the Deliverance and Inner Healing Session scheduled for me at_____ (Church) scheduled for date: _____.

Signature: _____ Date Signed: _____

*What was the main reason that prompted you to seek out inner healing or deliverance?

_____

_____

INNER HEALING/SPIRITUAL WARFARE QUESTIONNAIRE

DATE: _____ NAME: _____
AGE: _____ SEX: _____ RACE: _____ NATIONALITY: _____
ADDRESS: _____ STATE: _____ ZIP: _____
PHONE: _____ EMAIL: _____
CHURCH ATTENDING: _____ PASTOR'S NAME: _____
EMPLOYER/OCCUPATION: _____

PRESENT MARITAL STATUS:
(circle one)
SINGLE – MARRIED – SEPARATED – DIVORCED – REMARRIED – WIDOWED – LIVING TOGETHER

TOTAL # OF PREVIOUS MARRIAGES: _____ DIVORCES: _____
NUMBER OF KIDS: _____ NATURAL: _____ STEP &/OR ADOPTED: _____
NUMBER OF MISCARRIAGES _____ NUMBER OF ABORTIONS _____
PARENTS DIVORCED: Yes ___ No ___ HOW LONG: ____ (#yrs) BROTHERS & SISTERS: ____
PARENTS LIVING: Father: Yes ____ No _____ Mother: Yes ____ No _____
PARENTS SAVED: Father: Yes ____ No _____ Mother: Yes ____ No _____
PARTNER SAVED: Yes _____ No _____ PARTNER LIVING: Yes _____ No _____
Relationship with your parents (circle one):   Great   Good   OK   Bad   Indifferent
Relationship with your partner (circle one):   Great   Good   OK   Bad   Indifferent

CURSES OF THE WOMB
(circle one)
1a. Were you a planned child?   Yes   No   Don't know
    b.   Were you the "right" sex?   Yes   No   Don't know
    c.   Were you conceived out of wedlock?   Yes   No   Don't know
    d.   Were you adopted?   Yes   No   Don't know
    If so, do you know your biological parents?   Yes   No
    e. The result of violent conception?   Yes   No   Don't know
    f. Was your mother in a trauma during the pregnancy? Yes   No
2a. Was your child(ren) planned pregnancy?   Yes   No   Don't know
    b.   Was child(ren) cursed/unwanted?   Yes   No   Don't know
    c.   If so, by whom? (you, partner, parents): _____
    d.   If cursed, explain why? (i.e. wrong sex, bad timing, rape/violence):

_____
_____
_____
_____

ANCESTRAL (FAMILY) BACKGROUND – BLOODLINE RELATIVES

Look Up: Exodus 34:6-7; Numbers 14:18; Jeremiah 14:20
Circle and/or list below any negative qualities, problems, faults, disease/sickness and/or frequently reoccurring and/or repetitious patterns of negative emotions with **one word answer only** – pray first! No doubles needed; if acknowledged in part #1, no need to restate in part #2. No proper names, no sentences or phrases or positive words. Be honest with self (spiritual blindness & pride). For foster, adopted, and stepchildren do this section by faith; Best remembering those families that had greatest influences, upon your life.

INIQUITIES
Part 1

Circle the following patterns or frequently reoccurring activities your **family members** have been involved in:

Diseases/Sicknesses	Tobacco	Divorce
Bulimia/Anorexia	Alcohol/Drugs	Profanity
EasterStars/Freemasons/KKK	Gambling	Violence/Fighting
False Religions	Adultery/Fornication	Mental Illness
Child Abuse (Sexual/Physical)	Cults/Occult Groups	Anxiety/Breakdowns
New Age Movement	Pornography	Gluttony
Magic/Spiritism/Lucky Charms	Homosexuality	Secret Societies
Sexual Perversion / Incest, etc.	Racism/Bigotry	Scientology/Unitarian

List Others:_____

(Please list repetitious patterns below –Ex: rage, drugs, pride, anger, rejection, heart attacks)

MOTHER'S SIDE	**FATHER'S SIDE**

Grandparents

Parents

Brothers

Sisters

Aunts/Uncles

Cousins

BIBLICAL CURSES

Look Up: Galatians 3:13-14, Colossians 2:14; Deuteronomy 11:26-28;28:15

A curse may be defined as the uttering of a wish of evil against another—calling for harm, mischief, injury, or calamity to come upon someone. It includes acts of imprecation, harassment, torment, or the deliberate invoking of destruction or adversity.

You should never hesitate to break a curse over your own life. If you are mistaken, no harm is done. However, an unrecognized or unbroken curse can result in significant spiritual and practical consequences. Curses can function as spiritual strongholds, giving demonic forces legal grounds to operate.

Many people assert that they are not under any curses. In terms of final salvation, this is true. However, in the practical realities of daily life, believers can still be affected. These influences are not automatically removed at the moment of salvation. Some argue that because Jesus died to remove the curse, no believer could remain affected. Yet Scripture also tells us that Jesus died for the sins of the whole world (John 3:16). If redemption were automatic, all would be saved—but this is clearly not the case. The provision has been made and the price has been paid, but the benefits must be personally appropriated by faith.

In the same way, freedom from curses is available, but it must be intentionally received. Deliverance requires actively renouncing and breaking these legal grounds that allow demonic activity. Curses can have long-lasting, severe, and even catastrophic effects, making awareness and discernment essential.

Believers who walk in the knowledge and authority given to them in Christ are often especially targeted by the enemy. When curses are broken and returned to their source, as described in Psalm 109:17, there are repercussions in the spiritual realm.

Take time to pray and ask the Holy Spirit to reveal any areas that may apply to your life, and mark those that He brings to your attention.

BIBLICAL CAUSES OF CURSES

(You do not need to review Scriptures for #1-58, unless you don't understand terms)

1. Cursing Israel - Gen 27:29 / Gen 12:3 /Num 24:9
2. Willingly Deceiving Others - Josh 9:23 / Jer 48:10 / Mal 1:14
3. Adultery - Job 24:15-18 / Num 5:27 / Lev 20:10
4. Fornication - Deu 22:22-24
5. Doing the Lords Work Deceitfully - Jer 48:10
6. Rebellion Against Pastors - Deu 17:12
7. Disobedience to the Lord - Jer 11:3 / Deu 11:28 / Dan 9:11
8. Murder - Exodus 21:12
9. Rewarding Evil for Good - Prov 17:13
10. Pride - Psalms 119:21
11. Taking Advantage of the Handicapped - Deu 27:18
12. Not Giving to the Poor and Needy - Proverbs 28:27
13. Intercourse with Fathers Wife - Deu 27:20
14. Intercourse with sister or brother - Deu 27:22
15. Intercourse with Mother-In-Law - Deu 27:23
16. Intercourse with Daughter-In-Law - Lev 20:12
17. Intercourse with One of the Same Sex - Lev 20:13
18. Intercourse with Animals - Deu 27:21 / Lev 20:15-16
19. Intercourse During Menstruation - Lev 20:18
20. Sodomy/Anal Sex - Gen 19:13, 24-25
21. Rape - Deu 22:25-27

22. Marrying Both a Woman and Her Mother - Lev 20:14
23. Marrying a Sister - Lev 20:17
24. Kidnapping - Deu 24:7 / Ex 20:16
25. Striking Ones Parents - Ex 21:15
26. Cursing Ones Parents - Ex 21:1
27. Dishonoring Father or Mother - Deu 27:16
28. Causing the Unborn to Die / Abortion - Ex 21:22
29. Attempting to Turn Anyone Away from the Lord - Deu 13:6-9
30. Robbing God of Tithes and Offerings - Mal 3:9 / Haggai 1:6-10
31. Ministers who Fail to Give Glory to God - Mal 2:2 / Rev 1:6
32. Idolatry - Jer 44:8 / Deu 29:19 / Ex 20:5 / Deu 5:8-9
33. Keeping or Owning Cursed Objects - Deu 7:25-26 / Jos 6:18
34. Wickedness - Prov 3:33
35. Making a False Promise in the Lord's Name - Zech 5:4
36. Cheating People Out of Their Property - Deu 27:17
37. Making a Graven Image - Deu 5:8 / Deu 27:15 / Ex 20:4
38. Oppressing Strangers, Widows, & Orphans - Deu 27:19 / Ex 22:22-24
39. Slandering a Neighbor in Secret - Deu 27:24
40. Being a Thief - Zech 5:4
41. Taking Money to Kill the Innocent - Deu 27:25
42. Children Born from Incest - Gen 19:36-37 / Deu 23:3
43. Children Born Out of Wedlock - Deu 23:2
44. Curse Unborn Child - Deu 28:18, 53
45. Witchcraft - Ex 22:18
46. Following Horoscopes - Deu 17:2-5
47. Being a False Prophet - Deu 18:19-22
48. Not Staying a Virgin Until Married - Deu 22:13-21
49. Teaching Rebellion Against the Lord - Jer 28:16-17
50. Human Sacrifices - Lev 20:2
51. Participating in a Séance - Lev 20:6
52. Fortune Telling or Going to a Fortune Teller, Palmist, Tarot cards - Lev 20:6, 27
53. Being a Rebellious Child - Deu 21:18-21
54. Blaspheming the Lord's Name - Lev 24:15-16
55. Defiling the Sabbath - Ex 31:14 / Num 15:32-36
56. Doing Anything that is Punishable by Death - Deu 21:22-23
57. Prostitution - Prov 23:27-28
58. Addiction - Prov 25:28 / 1 Peter 5:8

Note:

1. Circle only what applies to YOU.
2. If you don't understand a topic, then look up the scripture pertaining to it.
3. Be honest. You only hinder your healing process by holding back.

BROKEN VOWS

Look Up: Numbers 30; Deuteronomy 23:21-22; Ecclesiastes 5:4-6; James 5:12

A vow is a promise. Scripture indicates that religious vows were regarded with great seriousness in the sight of the Lord. Therefore, broken vows can be a source of real trouble. That is why Jonah repented and renewed his vows in the belly of the whale saying, "I will pay my vows."

If a vow is found to be contrary to Scripture or dishonoring to God, it must be formally renounced and forgiveness sought after for having made it, in accordance with 1 John 1:9. Any vow that is inherently evil or made for an evil purpose should never be made or maintained. Upholding such a vow for the sake of consistency only compounds wrongdoing with further wrongdoing.

It is also important to recall and renounce any vows of consecration made to anyone or anything other than God—whether to a church, kingdom, organization, lodge, religion, family lineage, or even to parts of oneself or one's children.

Examples: Former marriages / broken engagements, broken fasts, broken promises to God, broken sobriety, broken financial commitments.

List Yours:

_____

_____

_____

NOTE: Broken vows are broken promises to God. Example: "Get me out of this mess, God & I'll go to church every Sunday."

Unhealthy Vows Made

There may be unhealthy vows or pacts made that will need to be broken. Ask the lord for forgiveness for making these unhealthy vows and orally renounce the forces of evil behind them.

Examples: Pact made with devil, blood pact/oath, vow to no longer let men hurt you (leads to mistrust), cults, vow made with the dead, vow to never trust again.

List Yours:

_____

_____

_____

SOUL TIES
1 Samuel 18:1

Just as the Bible describes King David and Jonathan's souls as being knit together (a godly soul tie), Satan's counterfeit of an evil soul tie exists whether it be sexual or phycological. Regardless, they are sources of trouble. **Because of this, they need to be renounced and broken.**

Examples: *Between saved and unsaved friends, business associates and associations, cults, intimate relationships, freemason/lodges, relatives, those formed by former engagements, former marriages, adultery and/or fornication, rape, incest, homosexual experiences, lustful crush on another, possessive or controlling parent or guardian, etc.*

Bow your head, close your eyes and ask the Holy Spirit to show you "<u>unhealthy</u> relationships or friendships" that you need to break free from. Ask forgiveness from the Lord and to break the hold they have over your soul.

Prayer: "If I'm not meant to have it Lord, please remove the desire from my heart to want it, and help me to find peace in it's absence."

<u>Remember to speak them out and list them below.</u>

Are you presently married or engaged? If so, break all ungodly soul ties between you two, in Jesus' name!

Notes: We will uncover a few soul ties today – Hosea 4:6 – My people (perish or are destroyed) because of lack of knowledge. During prayer time, let the Holy Spirit show you your past. You could be rebuking the Holy Spirit while he is intentionally bringing things to your mind he wants you to deal with, not the devil.

<u>List:</u>

Flesh Soul ties (ie. Past Sexual Partners, Rape, Organ/Blood Donor or Recipient):

_____

_____

_____

Psychological Soul Ties (ie. Loss of child/fetus, Relative or Pet, Broken friendship):

_____

_____

_____

DETESTABLE OBJECTS
Look up: Deuteronomy 7:26 and Acts 19:18-19

Bow your head, close your eyes and ask and allow the Holy Spirit to take you through each room, closet and drawer, etc. showing you the items that are unpleasing in God's sight. These are items that belong to you. If it belongs to your spouse, write it down and it is to be discussed to eliminate strife and division in the house. If you are in doubt about an item, write it down and allow others to aid you. For example, a form of Necromancy is: old love letters & dead relationships.

Home	Examples of Objects
Bedrooms	Sexual paraphernalia
Hallways	Jewelry Box (itself or items)
Kitchen	Love letters, tattoo that binds you
Dining Room	Magazines/books – Occult, sci-fi
Living Room	Foreign and domestic relics
Family Room	Pictures, CD's, mixed tapes, etc.
Bathroom	Statues (Buddha, infant of Prague, Mother Mary)
Basement	Rosary beads, sacred medals, icons
Attic	Carvings, magical trinkets, masks
Storage Room	Good luck charms, superstitious items
Chests	Demonic games, Ouija boards, Dungeons & Dragons
Drawers	Horoscope/Astrology/Zodiac, Tarot cards
Laundry Room	Ex's clothing, cologne, mementos
Closets	Snakes, witches, devil, demons, gargoyles
Yard	Dream catchers, totem poles, tikis

Other Objects:

FORGIVENESS
Look Up: Mat 5:22 / Col 3:13-15 / Matt 6:14-15 / Matt 18:21-34,35 / Eph 4:30-32

Willingness to forgive is absolutely essential for deliverance. **Forgiveness is not optional**; it is foundational. Unforgiveness toward oneself, toward God, or toward others can open the door to torment and spiritual bondage. Jesus calls us to live as He lived—a life marked by forgiveness. Even as He hung on the cross, He prayed, *"Father, forgive them, for they do not know what they do."*

Forgiveness can be difficult, especially when it requires extending grace to those who seem undeserving or hard-hearted. Releasing a wrongdoer rather than demanding what feels like a just penalty calls us to act in love, rejecting bitterness, resentment, and the desire for retaliation. This runs contrary to our natural inclinations.

Forgiveness does not mean forgetting the *wrong* that was done. It is not an emotion or a feeling, but a deliberate choice—an act of the will and a decision of faith. We forgive not because we feel like it, but because our future demands it. When we forgive, in the name of Jesus, it is settled and complete. Forgiveness is not mental striving or forcing ourselves into new thought patterns; it is a decision made in prayer.

The true issue is not whether we feel capable of forgiving, but whether we are willing to choose forgiveness. When we are willing, God promises to supply even the desire to change. Just as God has forgiven and forgotten our sins, we too must choose to forgive ourselves and release the past. The blood of Jesus is powerful enough to cleanse us from all guilt and shame.

Satan is a liar and the father of lies, and unforgiveness often disguises itself under different names—resentment, bitterness, anger, grudges, hatred, malice, envy, or thoughts of revenge. Though these may appear different, they all share the same root: unforgiveness.

Bow your head, and pray this prayer out loud, remembering to speak it out as the Holy Spirit recalls names, incidents, and people from your childhood to present. **Take your time - do not rush** – to cover each & every individual incident in your life. Do not list them.

Prayer: "Lord Jesus, I confess that I have held ill feelings and resentments against people (living or dead). I call upon You and ask You to help me to forgive myself, these people, groups, institutions, churches, and governments. I ask You Father, in the name of Jesus, by the power of the Holy Spirit, to drop in my mind and bring to my remembrance the name of anyone or anything, whose actions or words – real or imagined – hurt me, or another person for which I hold or have held ill feelings and resentments, hate, envy, malice, vengeance, unforgiveness, bitterness or grudges against. Father, as You forgave me when I did not deserve to be forgiven, so likewise I forgive – whether they deserve it or not – in Jesus' name."

NOTES: Go home & within the next 30 days, spend a total of **3 hours** forgiving. Forgiveness works 3 ways – God, self, others. Forgiveness is not a feeling, but a choice – the Devil influences emotions.

COMMUNION
Look Up: 1 Corinthians 11:23-30

The elements of Communion symbolically represent our Lord Jesus Christ as the "Passover Lamb who was sacrificed." By faith, we come into the very presence of the Lord and fellowship with Him because of the blood He shed at Calvary for the forgiveness of our sins. The Lord's Supper reminds us of the continual renewal of the covenant between God and His Church.

The word *remembrance* refers not only to our remembering the Lord, but also to God's remembrance of His redemptive work on our behalf through Jesus the Messiah—His covenant and His promise to restore the kingdom. When we partake of Communion, these truths are brought before God as an act of true intercessory prayer.

The bread represents Christ's body, broken for us, bearing our sins, iniquities, and transgressions, and granting us access to healing. Because of this, Christ's body heals us. The blood of Christ stands as the sign by which God remembers that we are in covenant with Him. Through the blood of Jesus, we are delivered and cleansed from all unrighteousness. Because of this, Christ's blood delivers us.

Our response is to live lives of obedience and holiness, pursuing a deeper and more intimate relationship with Christ. We are called to strive toward a life free from sin. The power of the blood of Jesus is such that when it is applied to our lives by faith, deliverance takes place immediately. No enemy or evil spirit—whether in heaven or on earth—can withstand the power of His blood.

At Calvary over two thousand years ago, Jesus completed His work by defeating sin, death, and the devil. We are called to act in faith and to use the spiritual weapons He has given us, including Communion. God invites us to the Lord's table to be refreshed in His presence and renewed in our commitment to Him. His mighty power is ready to heal and deliver.

Bow your head, search, and prepare your heart, <u>examine and judge yourself</u>, as you ask the Holy Spirit of God if you have any areas of <u>unconfessed sin</u> or <u>deliberate sin</u> in your life. Wait on Him and according to 1 John 1:9 ask and receive your forgiveness from Him. Say it aloud, remembering the power of the spoken word. 1 John 1:9 says, *"If we confess our sins, He is faithful and just to forgive us our sins, and to cleanse us from all unrighteousness."*

Communion Prayer: In the name of Jesus, I renounce all spiritual bondage and contamination from evil and I declare that every demonic entanglement and attachment is destroyed and removed from my life. I submit to the healing power of the broken body of Jesus, and the cleansing power of the blood of Jesus. I renounce all unconfessed sin in Jesus' name and ask you, Heavenly Father, to forgive me. Isaiah 53:5 says, *"For He was wounded for our transgression, He was bruised for our iniquities, the chastisement of our peace was upon Him, and by His stripes we are healed."*

INNER HEALING / LIFE-ALTERING STORIES

Pray and enter information about 5 most traumatic experiences, times, and situations in your life, in order of occurrence by age, if possible.

EXAMPLES: The one particular time you ever felt most rejected? Most embarrassed and ashamed? Broken and hurt emotionally? Most hate and anger? Bitter and resentful? Abandoned? Most scared or fearful?

==

==#1 HOW OLD WERE YOU? _____ WHO WAS INVOLVED? _____

FORGIVEN THEM? yes / no WHAT HAPPENED? (No more than 1-3 sentences)

_____

_____

LIST YOUR FEELINGS (single words only)

_____

==

==#2 HOW OLD WERE YOU? _____ WHO WAS INVOLVED? _____

FORGIVEN THEM? yes / no WHAT HAPPENED? (No more than 1-3 sentences)

_____

_____

LIST YOUR FEELINGS (single words only)

_____

==

==#3 HOW OLD WERE YOU? _____ WHO WAS INVOLVED? _____

FORGIVEN THEM? yes / no WHAT HAPPENED? (No more than 1-3 sentences)

_____

_____

LIST YOUR FEELINGS (single words only)

_____

==

==#4 HOW OLD WERE YOU? _____ WHO WAS INVOLVED? _____

FORGIVEN THEM? yes / no WHAT HAPPENED? (No more than 1-3 sentences)

_____

_____

LIST YOUR FEELINGS (single words only)

_____

==

==#5 HOW OLD WERE YOU? _____ WHO WAS INVOLVED? _____

FORGIVEN THEM? yes / no WHAT HAPPENED? (No more than 1-3 sentences)

_____

_____

LIST YOUR FEELINGS (single words only)

_____

SNARES/OPEN DOORS
Circle what applies to <u>YOU</u> & put "C" for Current, "P" for Past in front of snares. Gen 4:7

<u>AFFECTION</u>
Pretentious
Sissy/baby talk
Sophistication
Theatrics
<u>BITTERNESS</u>
Anger
Hatred
Resentment/Grudges
Retaliation
Temper
Unforgiveness
Violence
<u>BONDAGES/YOKES</u>
Addictions
Alcohol
Caffeine
Chains
Co-dependency
Compulsions
Compulsive Eating
Controlling others
Craving
Debilitating put-downs
Disorderliness
Drugs
Drunkard
Food/Gluttony
Gambling
Hunger
Infantile behavior
Impulsiveness
Medication
Narcotics
Neg attention-getting
Nervousness
Nicotine/smoking
Poor eating habits
Reckless driving
Reckless spending
Resentment
Self-rewarding
Tobacco
Toxic
Video games/internet

<u>BRUTALITY</u>
Child Abuse
Fighting
Malice/jealousy
Physical abuse
Rage/hurt
Revenge
Terrorism
Torment
Tough/violation
Vengeful
Violence
Wife-beater
<u>COMPETITION</u>
Argument
Compulsive
Drinking
Ego
Pride
Pushy
Ruthless
<u>CONTROL</u>
Charming
Dominance
Hypnotic
Manipulative
Objecting
Possessive
Witchcraft
<u>COVETOUSNESS</u>
Bribery
Discontent
Extortion
Graft
Greed/Mammon
Idolatry
Kleptomania
Lucifer
Materialism
Material lusts
Racketeering
Robber
Shopping
Stealing
Thief

<u>CRITICAL</u>
Accusation
Condemning
Exaggeration
Fault finding
Gossip
Judging
Name calling
Perfectionist
Ridicule
Verbal abuse
Verbal threatening
<u>CULTS/OCCULT</u>
Ancestor worship
Black magic
Charms/conjurer
Divination
False religions
Holistic
Horoscopes
Humanism
Hypnotism
Masonry/chains
Medium
Necromancy
New age
Paganism
Spiritism/animal spirit
TM/mysticism
Tarot cards/crystal ball
White magic
Witchcraft/Wicca
<u>DEATH</u>
Abortion
Murder
Suicide attempt
<u>DEPRESSION</u>
Defeatism
Dejection/despondency
Despair
Discouragement
Hinderance
Hopelessness
Insomnia
Morbidity

<u>DIVORCE</u>
Argument
Bickering
Contention
Discord
Disharmony
Divisiveness
Fighting
Spite
Strife
Quarreling
<u>DOUBT</u>
Skepticism
Unbelief
<u>ESCAPE</u>
Alcohol
Drugs
Indifferent
Passivity
Pacing
Restlessness
Rocking
Sleepiness
Stoicism
Walking away
<u>FALSE BURDEN</u>
False compassion
False peace
False responsibility
<u>FAMILY DESTRUCTION</u>
Family despair
Family embarrassment
Family hopelessness
Family shame
Alcoholic destruction
Child abuse
Childishness
Controlling others
Deaf ear to others
Dysfunctional family
Hatred of children
Poor communication
Lack of feeling
Lack of trust
Self-image destruction

FATIGUE
Captive
Chronic pain
Dyslexia
Laziness
Narcolepsy
Tiredness/exhaustion
Sleeplessness
Slothfulness
Sluggishness
Vertigo

FEAR OF ALL KINDS
Hysteria/panic attacks
Phobias

FEAR OF AUTHORITY
Child murder
Child sacrifice
Cursing
Deceit/lying
Fraud
Excuses
Insubordination
Unhealthy fear of God

GRIEF
Crying
Cruel
Heartache
Overwhelming
Sadness
Self-pity
Sorrow
Strife
Torment

GUILT
Condemnation
Embarrassment
Shame
Unworthiness

HEAVINESS
Burden
Disgust
Gloom & doom
Oppression

HYPERACTIVITY
Blocking
Driving
Distraction
Pressure
Restlessness

INDECISION
Compromise
Conformity
Confusion
Forgetfulness
Idleness
Indifference
Impaired judgement
Procrastination
Slow thinking
Stiffness
Stubborn

INFIRMITY
Anorexia/bulimia
Arthritis
Barrenness/miscarriage
Cancer
Deafness
Diabetes
Emotional
Emphysema
Epilepsy
Hypoglycemia
Necrosis
Nervous breakdown
Physical sickness
Migraines/mind binding
Multiple sclerosis

INHERITANCE
Drunken conception
Control
Curses
Emotional patterns
Iniquity
Negative Personalities
Physical hinderances
Traditions

IMPATIENCE
Agitation
Condemnation
Criticism
Frustration
Intolerance
Resentment
Self-awareness
Self-condemning
Unfair

INSECURITY
Deep insecurity
Forsakenness
Inadequacy
Inferiority
Loneliness
Neglect
Sadness
Self-pity
Shame
Timidity
Unfair
Worthlessness

JEALOUSY
Covet
Distrust
Envy
Selfishness
Suspicion

MIND BINDING
Confusion
Fear of failure
Fear of man
Incoherence
Intellectualism
Lack of concentration
Mind idolatry
Mispronunciation
Misspell
Misunderstand
Mix up
Occult spirits
Rationalization
Spiritism

NERVOUSNESS
Excitement
Headache
Insomnia
Nervous habits
Restless
Roving
Tension

NOISE
Deafness
Idle talk
Not being accepted
Silent
Talkativeness

PARANOIA
Cleanliness
Confrontation
Dirt
Distrust
Fears
Fetish
Filth
Envy
Jealousy
Mistrust
Persecution
Suspicion
Thoughts

PASSIVITY
Funk
Indifference
Lethargy
Listlessness
Sluggishness

PERFECTION
Anger
Criticism
Ego
False blame
False joy
Frustration
Know-it-all
Intolerance
Irritability
Pride
Self-centered
Self-favoritism

PERSECUTION
Degradation
Accusations
Fear of judgement
Sensitiveness
Unfairness

POVERTY
Barriers/walls
Blinders
Camouflages
Depravity
Entrapments
Evil alliances
Plagues
Stigmas
Yokes

PRIDE
Advertise
Attract attention
Babylonian
Blatancy
Bloated aristocrat
Boastful
Bombastic
Brazen
Center stage
Cocky
Colorful
Conceit
Condescension
Conspicuous
Crowd pleaser
Crude
Daring
Dazzle
Deadly sin
Demonstration
Domineering
Dramatics
Egotistic
Elate
Elaborate
Extravagant
Exhibition
Flagrancy
Flamboyant
Flashy
Gaudiness
Glare
Gorgeousness
Grandeur
Haughtiness
Hoity-toity
High-horse
Impressive
Inflate
Insolence
Kingly/queenly
Lavish
Limelight
Loftiness
Lordliness
Loudness
Luxurious
Me, myself & I

Narcissism
Obstinate
Obtrusive
Ostentatious
Over ambitious
Overbearing
Pageantry
Parade
Patronizing
Peacockery
Pompous
Presumptuous
Pride of position
Proud as lucifer
Proud hearted
Ritzy
Self-centered
Self-complacent
Self-exaltation
Selfish
Self-righteous
Self-satisfy
Sensationalism
Shameless
Showboat/show off
Spectacle
Stiff-necked
Strut
Stuck-up
Superbia
Superiority
Theatrics
Vanity
Vulgar

REBELLION
Anti-submission
Disobedience
Disrespectful
Dominant
Dominion
Evasive
Lawlessness
Nagging
Overbearing
Possessive
Rebel against God
Self-will
Stubborn
Temper tantrum

REJECTION
Fear of failure
Fear of rejection
Sensitive

RELIGIOUS
Atheism
Doctrinal error
Doctrinal obsession
False prophecy
False vision
Fear vision
Fear of God
Fear of Hell
Formalism
Hypocrisy
Legalism
Lost salvation fear
Religiosity
Relic/Pharisee
Ritualism
Sacred
Seduction
Self-righteousness

RETALIATION
Cruelty
Destruction
Explosion
Hatred
Hurt
Riling
Sadism
Selfishness
Spite
Violence

SELF-ACCUSATION
Self-comparison
Self-delusion
Self-seduction
Pride

SENSITIVENESS
Fear of disapproval
Fear of man
Self-awareness

SEXUAL IMPURITY
Adultery
Anal sex/sodomy
Exposure
Fantasy lust
Frigidity

Fornication
Homosexuality
Incest
Inflamed passions
Leacher
Lust
Masturbation
Molestation
Perversion
Pimp
Pornography
Promiscuous
Prostitute
Rape/violation
Roving eye
Sadomasochistic
Seducing
Sensual
Sex fantasy
Sexual immorality
Unclean
Untouchable
Violated
Whore

SPIRITUAL BLINDNESS
Blame
Deception
Denial
Distortion
Hindered watchfulness
Spiritual deafness
Unteachable

STRONGHOLDS (MIND)
Blurred mind
Boredom
Controlled insecurity
Confusion
Deep hurt
Deep insecurity
Delusion
Dense/lunatic
Emotional immaturity
Failure complex
Hallucinations
Holistic
Hypnotism
Immature thinking
Insanity
Lack of courage

STRONGHOLDS (cont.)

Low self-esteem
Madness
Mania
Melancholy
Mental illness
Mental instability
Mind binding
Mind blanking
Occult spirits
Retardation
Schizophrenia
Senility
Vain imagination

STRONGMEN
Bondage
Deaf & dumb
Dying/heaviness
Divination
Fear
Jealousy
Idolatry
Infirmity
Shame

TALE-BEARING
Back-biting
Belittling
Blasphemy
Coarse jesting/crude jokes
Gossip
Mockery/profanity
Cursing
Railing
Babbling

TESTING
Aggravating
Agitating
Belittling
Exhibiting
Foolishness
Initiating
Jeering
Mischievousness
Mocking
Sarcasm
Sneering

UNFORGIVING
Armor of mistrust
Bitter
Coldness

Ill feelings
Regret
Resentment
Ungrateful
Whiner

UNTOUCHABLE
Man-hater
Rape
Woman-hater
Violation

WITHDRAWAL
Daydreaming
Fantasy
Isolation
Pouting
Pretension
Unreality

WORRY
Apprehension
Anxiety
Dread
Fear/horror
Nightmares/night terrors
Scared
Torment

EXTRAS
Animalism
Blackouts
Communism
Confederate
Contentions
Debauchery
Delinquency
Hearing voices
Hallucinations
Hangovers
Irresponsibility
Liberalism
Losing jobs/unemployed
Pleasure
Racism
Red eyes
Rock music
Serpent
Shock
Suffering
Unfruitful
Unreliable

Chapter 12 — Inner Healing Leader Instruction

Supplies: communion cups, anointing oil, bucket (for potential vomiting), notebook/paper, pen/pencil, *The God Standard* Manual, completed Inner Healing packet, worship music & Kleenex.

1. **Opening Prayer:** *"Thank you, Jesus, for what You have already done in _____'s life. I ask that You lead _____ into freedom during this session. We invite the Holy Spirit to take control of this session and reveal to us what has been hidden in dark places. Father God, shed light onto these dark places so that _____ may be fully renewed. By the authority of Jesus Christ, I command the enemy to be silent. I ask the Lord to restore what the enemy has stolen and now fill _____ up with the Father's love, so that this becomes a place of healing, in Jesus' name. Amen."*

2. **Communion:**
   a. **Leader says:** *Jesus not only died for you, but as you. The body of Jesus makes us right-standing with God and the blood of Jesus washes away our sins, fulfilling the obligation of the law and makes us holy for the indwelling of the Holy Spirit.*
      i. **His Body**: *He was pierced for our transgressions (He died for our sins), He was crushed for our iniquity (His internal bleeding represented the generational curse all the way back to the fourth generation), the chastisement of our peace was upon Him (chastisement is condemnation under the law which sentences us to death. These judgments rendered us captive and Prov 26:2 says an undeserved curse cannot land on the righteous), and by his stripes, we are healed* (Break and eat the bread).
      ii. **His Blood**: Heb 9:22 says, *"Without the shedding of blood, there is no forgiveness of sins." We partake of the New Covenant in His blood. The blood the fulfills the obligation of the law by washing away our sins, generational curses, false accusations and judgments as well as sickness and disease* (Drink).

3. **Anoint** him/her with Oil (cross on forehead) and Ask the Holy Spirit to come upon him/her.
   a. **Leader says:** James 5:14-16, *"Is anyone among you sick? Let them call the elders of the church to pray over them and **anoint them with oil** in the name of the Lord. And the prayer offered in faith will make the sick person well; the Lord will raise them up. If they have sinned, they will be forgiven. Therefore, confess your sins to each other and pray for each other so that you may be healed. The prayer of a righteous person is powerful and effective."*
   b. Have the prayee/client **close their eyes** and keep their eyes closed throughout the rest of inner healing. This is a way of declaring, "I'm turning my attention away from the distractions of this world and toward God."

4. **Read Psalm 139** as a declaration over the Prayee. This is also used when someone has been cursed in the womb. **Psalm 139** says (verses 19-21 omitted), *"Lord, you know everything there is to know about _____. You perceive every movement of his/her heart and soul, and You understand his/her every thought before it even enters their mind. You are so intimately aware of him/her, Lord. You read his/her heart like an open book and You know all the words he/she is about to speak before they even start a sentence! You know every step he/she will take before his/her journey even begins. You've gone into his/her future to prepare the way, and in kindness you follow behind him/her **to spare him/her from the harm of his/her past**. With your hand of love upon his/her life, You impart blessing to him/her. This is just too wonderful, deep, and incomprehensible! Your understanding of him/her brings him/her wonder and strength. Where could we go from Your Spirit? Where could we run and hide from Your face? If we go up to heaven, You're there! If we go down to the realm of the dead, You're there too! If we fly with wings*

into the shining dawn, You're there! If we fly into the radiant sunset, You're there waiting! Wherever we go, Your hand will guide us; Your strength will empower us. It's impossible to disappear from You or to ask the darkness to hide him/her, for Your presence is everywhere, bringing light into his/her night. There is no such thing as darkness with You. The night, to You, is as bright as the day; there's no difference between the two. You formed _____ in his/her innermost being, shaping his/her delicate inside and his/her intricate outside, and wove them all together in his/her mother's womb. I thank You, God, for making _____ so mysteriously complex! Everything You do is marvelously breathtaking. It simply amazes us to think about it! How thoroughly You know _____, Lord! You even formed every bone in his/her body when You created him/her in the secret place, carefully, skillfully shaping him/her from nothing to something. You saw who you created _____ to be before he/she became into being! Before he/she ever saw the light of day, the number of days You planned for him/her were already recorded in your book. Every single moment You are thinking of him/her! How precious and wonderful to consider that You cherish him/her constantly in Your every thought! O God, Your desires toward _____ are more than the grains of sand on every shore! When I awake each morning, You're still with him/her...God, we invite Your searching gaze into _____'s heart. Examine him/her through and through; find out everything that may be hidden within him/her. Put him/her to the test and sift through all his/her anxious cares. See if there is any path of pain he/she is walking on, and lead him/her back to Your glorious, everlasting ways— the path that brings him/her back to You, in Jesus' name."

      a.   **Cursed in womb?** (refer to their packet, pg 5) If he/she was an unwanted pregnancy, opposite sex of what was desired, or ever thoughts of termination of the pregnancy, take the client through this: *"Holy Spirit help _____ to go back to the time before he/she was conceived. Know your parents, no matter who they are, were chosen. Eph 1:4 tells us: 'Even before He made the world, God loved us and chose us in Christ to be holy and without fault in His eyes.' Hear Jesus, even now, calling your name, _____. You need to know that your God rejoiced in the day that you were conceived. He wanted you and delighted in your conception. We live in a fallen world. Our parents have faults and failures that were not part of God's original plan for their lives. But the Lord was very much involved, no matter how your parents felt about it. You are exactly the person God wanted. You were never a mistake or an accident in His eyes. Are you willing to forgive your parents for cursing you in the womb?"*

If they can answer yes to that last question, have client **repeat** back: *"In the name of Jesus, I declare over myself that I was chosen. My birth has always been the Lord's desire. I release my parents into your hands Lord, and I ask for their forgiveness. I give these curses up to you Lord, and I ask that you remove them from my life forever, in Jesus' name."*

      b.   **Child cursed in womb?** (refer to their packet, pg 5) Break curse words off your child(ren). **Repeat:** *"Father, I come to you, in the name of Jesus, and I break every ill feeling or curse of words against _(child's name)_. I take every word captive that has been spoken over _(child's name)_. I break the power of those curses as my children and I are no landing path for a curse. I cancel every assignment of darkness and I cast them to the ground to be without effect. I call blessings to fall on my family in its place. I bless your existence, _(child's name)_, with love, peace, joy, acceptance, and excitement! I plead the blood of Jesus over my family to stand as a wall of separation between us and the enemy. Holy spirit, come into my life and fill every place the enemy once occupied, in Jesus' name. Amen."*

  5. **Ancestral (Family) Background:** (refer to their packet, pg 6) Leader read and have them repeat iniquities/curses that they have circled and/or listed.

      a.   **Break Family or Familial Spirit:** Have prayee **repeat** back prayer: *"Father, I come to You, in the name of Jesus, thanking You for Your Word and the Holy Spirit that has made me aware of my sin. I renounce the Familial Spirit and ask that You, Lord Jesus, forgive* *me and my family of any past or current involvement in occult activities. I love You, God, and I want to live a life that is pleasing to You. I declare that Jesus is the way, the truth, and the life. No one comes to the Father but through Him. Jesus is Lord of all and I worship Him, and Him alone. Satan, in the name of Jesus, I bind you, your **Familial Spirit** and its demons according to Matthew 18:18, which gives me authority to bind and loose on earth as it is in Heaven. By the blood of Jesus, I sever any and every entanglement, attachment and pact that was made either by me or my family in the past, and I plea the blood of Jesus as a wall of separation between us. Devil, you have no hold on my heart and life or that of my family from now on, in the name of Jesus. Thank You, Lord Jesus, for freeing me. Give me a deep desire to pursue you and your truth for the rest of my life. In the name of Jesus, I loose the power of the Holy Spirit in my life to restore me and my family, and fill every place that enemy once occupied and influenced."*

      b.   Prayer counselor closes the door, binding spirits just listed: *"Father, I come to You, in the name of Jesus, and I bind every spirit tied to these family curses and their demons and I break their hold over _____ (person's name) so that when they are cast out, they will not come back. I break the power of every curse that he/she has released over someone's life or that he/she has received in his/her heart. In the name of Jesus, I command you to loose him/her and let him/her go. I close every door that you have used to access his/her heart and life and I plead the blood of Jesus over that door as a wall of separation between you. Holy Spirit, come into his/her life and fill every place in his/her heart that was once occupied and influenced by the enemy. In Jesus' name, Amen."*

    6. **Prayer to Renounce Personal Confessions** (refer to their packet, Curses pgs 8-9 & Snares at end) Leader: Read circled items from both sections and ask them to **repeat each one** after you. This is a time for repentance, meaning to return back to God.

      a.   Leader reads, client to **repeat**: *"Dear Father, if I have believed, accepted, taught, taken part in teachings or practices contrary to Your will or Your Word, or in any other way been displeasing to You, I am truly sorry. I ask You to forgive me, in the name of Jesus Christ. I hereby renounce these things, Lord, in the name of Jesus Christ, and under His precious blood. With Your help, I promise You, I will not engage in them anymore."*

      b.   **Generational & Personal Curse Declaration:** Leader to read, client **repeats** back: *"Heavenly Father, according to my covenant with you, I ask You to open the books of my past, and of every covenant made by my forefathers that they entered into on my behalf that is giving protection to the demonic around me. Look at these sins, Heavenly Father, and see if any of these are not absolutely just and righteous. Then annul them and release the affliction of the demonic on me."*

      c.   **Counselor Closes the Door on Personal and Generational Curses:** *"In the name of Jesus, we declare the blood of Jesus to stand between him/her and the fourth, third, second and first generation as a wall of separation. I cancel every assignment of darkness and remove every right of the demonic to afflict _____ because of the known or unknown sins of previous generations. I call to him/her only righteous inheritance and the blessings of previous generations."*

    7. **Broken Vows:** (refer to their packet, page 10) Read and have them **repeat** listed vows, then repeat: *"Dear Father, if I have believed, accepted, taught, taken part in teachings or practices contrary to Your will or Your Word, or in any other way been displeasing to You, I am truly sorry. I ask You to forgive me, in the name of Jesus Christ, for breaking any godly vows. I hereby renounce unhealthy vows made, in the name of Jesus Christ, and under His precious blood. With your help, I promise You, I will not engage in these vows anymore."*

    8. **Soul Ties & Idols:** (refer to their packet, pgs 11-12) Discuss what Psychological and Sexual Soul Ties represent. Ask who else they may have soul ties with? Did they donate blood/organs or were recipient of blood/organs. If so, break the fleshly tie and call blessings onto

both parties instead of curses that may be attached. Have client read names listed on page 11. Read their Detestable Objects on page 12 and discuss the importance of cleansing or purging those items from their home that may link to those soul ties.

a. Breaking sexual soul ties: Read and have them **repeat**: *"In the authority of Jesus, I plead the blood of Jesus to stand between me and every sexual soul tie listed and any others I may not remember at this time to separate the "one flesh" union. I send back to them* [or re-list names] *everything that I have taken from them/him/her in the one flesh union and I call back to me everything that I gave to them/him/her in that union. I declare the blood of Jesus to be a wall of separation between us. Thank You Jesus for restoring my soul."*

b. Breaking psychological soul ties: Read and have them **repeat**: *"Lord Jesus, I thank you that you carried my grief and my sorrows so I would not have to. Forgive me for believing the lies and allowing the enemy to torment me and gain ground in my heart through my loss. I lift up every psychological soul tie to You and release them into Your hands. Your word is the sword of the Spirit with the power to divide all things that oppose Your knowledge and Your will for my life. In the name of Jesus, I sever every demonic entanglement and attachment to all wrongful emotional, mental, spiritual and physical ties with these people* [or re-list names]. *I plead the blood of Jesus to stand as a wall of separation between us. Holy Spirit, I receive Your oil of joy instead of mourning and a garment of praise instead of a spirit of despair. Come into my heart and life and fill me in every place the enemy once influenced and occupied, in the mighty name of Jesus."*

c. **Forgiveness: Repeat** *"In the name of Jesus, I choose to forgive as I have been forgiven. I now choose to forgive the people that I created ungodly soul ties with. I release any right I have retained to bring revenge. I release them from my hands and place them into Your hands, Jesus, my Just Judge. I break every curse I have sent to them and call forth a blessing to them instead. Thank you for the grace to forgive and the power to live in freedom."*

d. **Forgiving God: Repeat** *"Father, I come to You in the name of Jesus and I thank You for being faithful in Your love towards me even when I was faithless. Forgive me for mistakenly believing the lies for what the enemy, or others under his direction, have done to me. You said You will never leave me nor forsake me and I know this is the truth. I have never been left alone and have never been forsaken. Thank You that these barriers I placed between us are now removed. I thank You for Your mercy and grace and ask that You help me to love You more and with that love, walk in a deeper more intimate relationship with You, in Jesus' name. Amen."*

Take 5 minute break

9. **Inner Healing/Life-Altering Stories:** (refer to their packet, page 15)

a. Dialog about their Traumatic Stories. Explain, *There is a demonic spirit known as 'memory recall,' which keeps wounds and trauma alive inside us. This demon torments a victim by keeping the painful memories of those past wounds alive. This is where we need to hand over those memories to Jesus.* (paraphrased by Frank Hammond, *Overcoming Rejection*)

b. Read each incident and ask them to describe the event in further detail.

c. *"How did it make you feel?"* Leaders, identify/list the negative emotions (lies)...write down one-word answers.

d. *"Ask the Holy Spirit to show you where Jesus is... what is He doing and what you see? Can you feel his presence?"* This is where we search for the truth. If none can be found, let them know they were not alone and Jesus loves them. If they cannot see Jesus, ask if they can feel or know that Jesus is there with them? Write down what they experience Jesus is doing and saying (identify truths). Discuss the **truths** with the client.

      i.   **Repeat:** *"I renounce the Lies [name each emotion], every tie, entanglement and attachment, and command it to leave my life, in the name of Jesus."*

          1. If it was **caused by another,** repeat: *"In the name of Jesus, I renounce all spirits of [name each **spirit**] that took over me because of [name the person who caused it and reason]. I forgive [names] and ask You to bless them, in the name of Jesus."*

      ii.   *"Were there any negative agreements or vows created?"* Renounce the agreement/vows the same way as the lies. Remember, as the person renounces each one, Leader breaks the tie, entanglement and attachment.

      iii.   Now go back and briefly reflect the incident. We are looking for negative emotions that are still attached. Ask how they feel now? If they don't feel peace, go back to "9c" and explore a little more.

      iv.   **Optional** forgiveness/verbal release declaration: *"Through Jesus, I forgive _____ for what I experienced. I won't hold this against _____ any longer. Even though my flesh wants vengeance, Lord, I know it is Your will that I forgive to be released from demonic entanglements and attachments. Father, in the same manner that You have forgiven me of all my offenses, I choose now to forgive my offender. I release _____ into Your hands. I give up every right to harbor resentment against them. I also ask for forgiveness for receiving the lie and I ask for forgiveness for feeling _____ (be specific). You said you would never leave me nor forsake me; I am Your son/daughter and nothing can separate me from Your love. I close the doors to the wounds of my past and I plead the blood of Jesus over it as a wall of separation between us. Thank you, Jesus, that your blood has cleansed me from all sins. Help me to bring my emotions into my alignment with my choice to forgive and to live a life that will honor You, in Jesus' name."*

      v.   Once they feel at peace, close the door... **Leader declares:** *"In the name of Jesus, I take authority over the spirit(s) of [name them], I bind them and I break every tie, entanglement and attachment and I plea the blood of Jesus over the door of _(prayee's name)_ heart. In Jesus' name, Amen."* Do this for each incident.

10. They are ready for Deliverance – Determine which spirits are attached to the emotions identified during this session.

Take 5 minute break

Deliverance

    Now that every vow/tie has been broken, the prayee/client must open their eyes and **keep their eyes open** throughout deliverance. The eyes are the windows to the soul and the spirits involved will be easily identifiable.

    1. **Binding Spirits:** If there are only a couple identified, use specific prayers assigned in Empowerment Training Manual. For more than 3 spirits to bind, use structure below. **Declare:** Read and **repeat** with prayee: *"I come to You now, Lord, as my deliverer. You know my special needs, and the things that bind, torment and defile as those evil, unclean spirits. I claim the promise of Your word, 'whosoever that calleth on the name of the Lord shall be delivered.' I call upon You now. In the name of Jesus, deliver me and set me free. Satan, I renounce you and all your works. I loose myself from you, in the name of Jesus, and I command you to leave me right now!"*

    2. **Optional Breakthrough Prayers:** If you have other various declarations that the prayee can read on his/her own, this would be a good time to go after specific "strongmen" or spirits through prayer.

3. **Take Authority:** *"Father in the name of Jesus, I take authority of the spirits of [name every spirit incurred from **all traumas**]. I bind them and break every tie, entanglement and attachment. Now that every matter is settled, in the name of Jesus, I cast you out of _____'s life and forbid you to return!"* Continue to command each spirit out as you see fit as it/they may manifest.

a. Once this is done, look into their eyes and see if it is gone. If you are unsure, always ask the client how they feel emotionally and physically. Remember, you are working together.

b. If the spirit you are commanding is still there, "prime the pump." Tell them to blow out as you cast the spirits out. They may cough or even vomit (into the bucket provided).

c. If, after several attempts, this does not help, more than likely you missed something. Pray, *"Holy Spirit, whatever issue is preventing their freedom, reveal it, in the name of Jesus."* Once it is revealed, the client goes through the process of renouncing it and leader goes through the process of taking authority over it, binding it and casting it out.

d. Continue to go through this process until the person is cleansed. Once clean, lead the client/prayee into giving thanks to God for Deliverance... Revelation 7:12 says, *"Praise and glory and wisdom and thanks and honor and power and strength be to our God for ever and ever. Amen!"*

e. **Give Praise:** Lead the them to Praise & Pray for the Fullness of the Holy Spirit. Prayee says, *"Lord Jesus, I give You thanks because You have delivered me. I now receive the anointing, the presence, the power and the grace of Your Holy Spirit. Now, fill me in every place the enemy once influenced and occupied, in Jesus' name. Amen."* After this prayer, you may see the Holy Spirit reveal other demons lingering through discernment or had the client say there is something else still there. If this is the case, go back to Step 2 in Deliverance, take authority over it and cast it out.

f. If they have physical disabilities, pray for their healing. If the physical disability has been a prolonged disability, have the client renounce the spirit of infirmity, and break its tie, entanglement and attachment. Leader binds it, breaks it and casts it out.

g. Once finished, remember to **De-Slime** after prayee leaves: *"Lord Jesus, I plead the blood of Jesus over my life and over the lives of my family. I ask that you cleanse me with Your blood and I hereby cancel any assignment of hell, and release the assignments of heaven over our lives. Lord Jesus, bless me and keep me by keeping my mind pure, help me to guard my emotions against anything that would come against my knowledge of you, protect my body from sickness and disease and I bless those who would curse me, in Jesus' name."*

h. Client may need follow-up mini sessions if he/she is not seeing resolve after the session and a 30-day post-care period. Keep in touch with the client for the following month. Encourage altar calls each Sunday for at least that post-care month.

i. Be available by phone or connect them to a member of your church that can be an assigned mentor. This will be key in maintaining their freedom.

Galatians 5:1 (NIV) proclaims, *"It is for freedom that Christ has set us free. Stand firm, then, and do not let yourselves be burdened again by a yoke of slavery."*

www.ingramcontent.com/pod-product-compliance
Lightning Source LLC
Chambersburg PA
CBHW080546090426
42734CB00016B/3215